Oldest on the Bus a  ne Cox. We are both in our ad a love of travel. Over ore adventurous and nov ents ourselves, so much n om a brochure! What start , ..eaks around Europe, expanded to a fortnights holiday in Vietnam, before redundancy opened up the opportunity for this four and a half months adventure.

The Oldest on the Bus name came from our travels around Thailand, Cambodia and Vietnam, where it was a running joke that we were always the oldest, surrounded by young backpackers almost half our age. We even created a blog for our second visit and subsequent travels around Nepal, Malaysia and Borneo, that can be followed at the following address...

https://oldestonthebus.home.blog/

The diaries that you are about to read were originally jotted down in a pale blue exercise book, destined solely to collect dust on a shelf. It was my Auntie Doreen who convinced us that they would be an interesting read, so with time on our hands the task of writing them up began. It seems that people have enjoyed reading them, so six months or so later a rejig, tidy up and a few photographs have been added to the original book ...

Also in the Middle-Aged Travel Adventures series...

Our Travels Around India

Backpacking...
Not Just For The Young!

Thailand : Cambodia

Vietnam : India

Preface

It all starts off as a 'what if' over a glass of red wine, usually after another stressful day at work. We both work for the same company that is fast going down the pan. Day after day working at a printing company with no paper but plenty of angry customers; they want their orders, so forced to lie, deceive and try to placate them whilst just hoping tomorrow will be better...

Something must give; we mull over the scenarios most evenings. Redundancies are unlikely – they have no money to pay redundancy. Will someone else take over part or all of the company? Could it just close? Although we both work here, we are in the fortunate position that money worries wouldn't be our immediate concern. Night after night the same conversations occur – not just about the desperate work situation, but the 'what if' – in the worst-case scenario would we dare to follow our dreams and go travelling around South East Asia?

Over our ten years together we have made plenty of visits to that part of the world, mainly to India but we have also visited Thailand, Vietnam and Sri Lanka along the way. We love the spicy food and their way of life; hectic, noisy, colourful, and smelly at times, but our overriding memories are of the people, so relaxed, happy and friendly. What we also know from our previous visits over the years is just how much further your money goes in this part of the world.

Whenever we were away in Asia we had often spoken to other tourists and been amazed that we seemed to be the only ones doing the routine fortnight's holiday - they were staying for months at a time! In India it would normally be people older than us. Why contemplate English winters when you can have sun every day, enjoy the beach or pool, dine out each night and feel so much happier and healthier due to all the sunshine? When we had been in Thailand or Vietnam it had been a younger crowd – often Australians. They would be on gap years, travelling around until their money had run out, exploring the world before settling down to more grown-up stuff. We were envious of both generations.

Travelling is definitely in our plans for the future; realistically once we have reached retirement... But what if that opportunity were to come along sooner? Our parents are all still alive, getting on a bit but in good health. Our daughter is coming up to twenty-one but has already settled down and is living with her boyfriend. With both of us employed by the same company what if we are suddenly without jobs?

Could we? Dare we? – it is easy talking it through and dreaming over a couple of glasses of wine.

The Opportunity Arises

Thursday the twenty-ninth of July, 2015. It seems like any other Thursday, soon to be Friday and another week done. Payday had been on the twenty-fifth and the money had gone in the bank. I, Wayne, sat within the accounts department and was always aware of how tight the cashflow around pay day has been for the last few months. The rumour spreading around the factory floor was that we have had our last payday, and that today is the day.

Over the last few months the notice boards have been awash with people who are leaving. The office is now made up of people who are either long serving or of apprentices getting their first experience of working life. It seems that anyone who had only a handful of years' service has already left for pastures new and hopefully a brighter future. It is only the security blanket of long service that is keeping the rest of us here.

The morning passes but there is an uneasy feeling. Over the last week or two there has been a lot of 'strange' faces around the place, no one is ever introduced to them but walking past the boardroom the number of them seems to rise daily. This Thursday it is like a mini-bus full of them has arrived, maybe ten or twelve of them in total? I leave for lunch as normal. On my return I am immediately informed that there is to be a meeting of all employees at 1 p.m. It is obviously important as most people would normally head out for lunch at that time, they have been told to wait. It is also shift change time for the factory, so the morning shift are due to leave and the afternoon shift set to start. Everyone is to meet in one of the old office areas that is no longer in use. The room gradually fills up as people who have had early lunches return and the afternoon shift arrives for work.

One fifteen arrives and goes; nothing. One thirty, still nothing. Some guy from the shop floor heads into the factory needing to go to the toilet, not familiar with where the office ones are. In no time he returns, the factory has been locked up. By now most people fear the worst. Wherever you worked in the company you knew things were bad. Reel porters had no paper to take to the presses. Press operators are stood around, having nothing to print on. Despatch operatives with nothing to send out the door. Over the last two weeks the customer services team have even been advised to point customers into the direction of alternative suppliers.

It is nearly two o' clock when the Managing Director comes in to brief everyone about what is happening. It is brief as well, the company has been put into administration and that is it, good-bye. He promptly leaves the room. One of the 'strange' faces then takes over the briefing, advising us all of what we need to do next – the company has gone into administration, you now need to claim redundancy through the government, the job centre is already aware of the situation and they would be doing all they can for you. Suddenly it is no longer a normal Thursday.

Once this guy has finished talking and handing out leaflets with phone numbers and websites that we will need, we are told to wait until our names are called out. Section by section we are taken back to our desks, lockers for the factory people, and watched over like hawks before being escorted off the premises. Alison, aged forty-eight, a Customer Service Manager and with twelve years' service, and Wayne, aged forty-five, IT Support and twenty-six years' service no longer have jobs.

Today, as the doors have been closed, and locked, on our place of work, others have opened...

We only live just around the corner from work, a five-minute bike ride through the cemetery. Alison had been escorted off twenty minutes or so before me, I biked down that driveway alone and off the company premises for a final time - it was a weird feeling, not one of sadness, but more of excitement. Whatever happened next would be a new chapter, neither of us had been enjoying work the last eighteen months but were not brave enough just to quit. Anyhow, we had been expecting something along these lines, so by sticking it through to the bitter end we had secured some redundancy – more than enough to cover our much talked about dreams.

That afternoon seemed to disappear in no time, a complete blur with lots of mixed feelings. Although we were financially stable, we appreciated that not everyone else was, so what was an exciting opportunity for us was a frightening time for others. After dropping a few texts to various family members and close friends it dawned on us, there was nothing in the way to stop our much talked about trip. Often when we mulled it over a glass of wine, we thought it might have been bought out by another company, or one of us would keep our jobs etc. etc.

That evening we meet up with a few of our friends who this afternoon had also become our ex-work colleagues. There is not a lot of sadness about the events, everyone had seen it coming. The worst thing about the situation is that a lot of hard-working people have had their lives turned upside down. It turns into a drunken and extremely late night; the beer keeps flowing until the early hours. Lots of memories and people from the past are talked about. There is a sense of shock around the town, not just from the people who had worked there - in Boston it has been a big employer for the last one hundred and fifty plus years.

August 2015

In our heads we know that we are going travelling, we have mentioned it since being made redundant to both sets of parents and our daughter, Lauren. Lauren thinks we are having a mid-life crisis, we see it more as an opportunity that is just too good to turn down. If we didn't do it now after all that talking over glasses of wine or cups of coffee on a Sunday morning then there would come a day when we would look back in later years and regret it.

Daily we switch the computer on and use the internet for tips and advice; we soon have various travel blogs bookmarked. We make a visit to the travel agents in town to collect some brochures and look at various routes that they are using on multi-centre holidays. We use Skyscanner's to look into prices of flights, Hotels.com for accommodation and Tripadvisor for reviews; cost wise it is all very much within our budget. From the travel blogs there is nothing that unnerves us, they are full of suggestions, recommendations and warnings - but all seem to concur with our thoughts, use common sense, keep your wits about you and we would be fine.

We already have flights booked for Thailand, this was going to be an eleven-night holiday, a few days in Bangkok then onto Chiang Mai – booked in the days when we only had twenty-six days annual leave each year! Those flights had been booked at a great price but on a non-refundable, non-changeable basis, so we looked at our travel insurance to see how we stood on that. It turns out that the insurance does cover redundancy, but the excess on the flight refund and the fact that it does not refund the air passenger duty part means that we would not get much back. Further searching and our minds are made up – rather than cancel that flight we go out on it as planned, so the twenty-eighth of October 2015 will be the start of our adventure. Heathrow to Bangkok, via Doha will be the first of many flights that we will be using over the next few months.

With our start date confirmed, when will we return? For us there is an obvious date - we need to be back for Alison's Mum and Dads sixtieth wedding anniversary, a party is already pencilled in for March the twentieth 2016. My own parents would be celebrating their fiftieth the following weekend, so with these occasions in mind we search for our return flight. We have already decided that we will be ending up in Goa, so onto Skyscanner's we go. We soon find a flight, at a decent price as well; Goa Dabolim to Heathrow via Oman with Oman Airways. We do a little bit of research into Oman airways having never used them before, fortunately all complimentary reviews and it is well ranked in the Skytrax airline awards too.

Now is the decisive moment, up until now it is still all talk, still just dreams, the research and speculation have been done but cost us nothing. Booking this flight from Goa to Heathrow will be making it real, costing us money, we must be certain. We look at each other, neither of us can think of a good reason not to do it. If we needed to get home quickly for any reason then that is not a problem, there is no reason though that we think that scenario would be likely. Feeling both nervous and excited at the same time we push the button 'book flights'... nothing happens other than a refusal from the Halifax bank! Within moments of our card being declined for payment, the phone rings. It is the Halifax, they suspect our card, or at least our card details, are being used fraudulently to book a flight through Oman Air. We confirm that no, it is us and we are looking to book that flight and will be looking at booking others over the next few days as well. That obstacle now overcome; a single ticket each for Goa to Heathrow for the thirteenth March 2016 sets our return date. That is four and a half months, the best part of twenty weeks, one hundred and thirty-eight days; we have only ever done a fortnight before!

With the start and end dates decided the rest could be planned around that. We know we are starting in Bangkok and ending in Goa, we also want to visit Cambodia and Vietnam during that time as well. Thailand we have been to once before, we had a wonderful time previously and wanted to spend more time in Bangkok. Last time it had been a whistle-stop tour, just ticking off the highlights from the guide book. Vietnam, likewise, but as recently as April; dashing around visiting the 'must see' attractions. This time we would be able to do it at a leisurely pace, really get a feel for the place. Cambodia and especially Angkor Wat have been on our list to do for a couple of years now. We had already considered visiting Angkor from Bangkok whilst we were on our original eleven-night holiday! Angkor Wat, one of the world's most iconic sights must be on our itinerary. A visit to Varanasi had always eluded us on our previous trips to India, its location is not the easiest to get to, this time there is no excuse.

Before we go any further and spend more money on flights etc. travel insurance is a must. We already have annual travel insurance in place, but due to the length of time that we will be away it is not valid. There is good advice in blogs and forums regarding visits to Cambodia; it is not the place to have an accident and require medical care. The general rule of thumb is that if you are touring around Cambodia ensure that your policy has 'Medevac' cover. This means that in case of an accident your policy covers evacuation across the border into Thailand, usually Bangkok, for any treatment. With this in the back of our minds we make sure that the cover on the policy is up to the job, like most insurance policies you hope that you will never require it, but it would be foolish to ignore such sound advice.

We soon discover via hotel booking sites that Thailand is far more expensive for accommodation than both Cambodia and Vietnam. Having already done the beach side of Thailand a few years previously, should we just stay in Thailand long enough to do Chiang Mai, our flights for there are already booked? We soon reach that conclusion, it is the cultural side of Thailand that we want to see, the beach part can wait until our time in Cambodia and Goa. We decide that we will have another couple of days in Bangkok on our return from Chiang Mai before leaving Thailand and moving onto Cambodia.

Our route through Cambodia will be as per blogs from the internet; Siem Reap for Angkor Wat and the Tonie Sap Lake - the largest freshwater lake in the whole of South East Asia. From Siem Reap, moving west and slightly southwards onto Battambang, for its famous Bamboo Train but also its history from the Pol Pot years. After Battambang continue south to the capital Phnom Penh. Phnom Penh is home to the notorious genocide sites and the most famous of the Killing Fields - all very grim, but if you travel to Cambodia something that cannot be ignored. From Phnom Penh we also plan to visit Kampot, home to the world's finest pepper, then perhaps Kep or Sihanoukville – Cambodia's beach resorts. All our travelling through Cambodia will be by road, we look at the Giant Ibis website, the most frequently mentioned bus company in blogs and on Tripadvisor. Prices for travel between the key cities is cheap, we just need to work out how long we need to spend in each place first though.

Phnom Penh is also the perfect place to cross the border into Vietnam, Ho Chi Minh City (HCMC) is just a six-hour coach journey away. We loved HCMC from our stay there in April, this time we would make our visit longer. We plan to do a similar route to what we crammed into our fortnights holiday previously, only this time we have time on our side. From HCMC we will visit Can Tho, Can Tho is the largest Vietnamese town on the Mekong delta. Again, we had visited earlier in the year when due to a disastrous journey from HCMC we had arrived in darkness and had to leave for a flight by midday! Following Can Tho we would visit Hoi An where we plan to celebrate Christmas. Hoi An is a stunning trading port, a world heritage site, that has the bonus of being by some lovely beaches. It is the finest preserved of all South East Asia's ancient trading ports – dating right back to the fifteenth century. From Hoi An it will be up to Hanoi, where we plan to visit the Sapa Mountains from, rather than Halong Bay which we have already done. The plan is to spend New

Year's Eve in Hanoi, before moving onto Goa in India early in the new year.

Goa is our favourite holiday destination; we have already been six or seven times in the past. Over the years we have managed to visit the Golden Triangle (Delhi, Agra (for the Taj Mahal) and Jaipur), Udaipur and Jodhpur in Rajasthan, Mumbai, Amritsar (the Golden Temple), Bangalore and Mysore. Up until now Varanasi has always been impossible, or at least exceedingly difficult due to flight schedules; this time with so much time to play with it will be possible even if we must stay overnight elsewhere on route each way. We have made some great friends in Goa, over the years we have used Valerie Travels for all our excursions, and in the last few years Valerie, Savio and their daughter Sovann have become close friends and a tremendous help to us when visiting Goa and planning places we want to visit. We are quick to let them know about our upcoming stay, two whole months rather than the usual fortnight. They are excited about our visit as they didn't think we would be coming this year, but going to Thailand instead.

Over the next few weeks we look at booking the necessary flights. Our plan is that we will depart Bangkok on or near to the date that what would have been our return flight home to England. With not having to stick to specific dates we can save a little by booking flights on days when they are cheapest. By now we have a rough idea of how long we wish to stay in each location for, all based on research and reviews of what there is to do in each area.

We find that once we book the flight to Siem Reap, the next month of travelling through Cambodia can be very flexible, all our movements will be by bus and can be booked once we arrive there. Looking further ahead we come across our first hiccup - there are no direct flights from Hanoi to Goa. With that being the case, we now need to find the most cost-effective route – one to have a ponder over! Meanwhile Valerie in Goa has been in touch with the option of an apartment very close to her new office. She knows from our past visits that we are always on foot and what area of Calangute we like, it sounds perfect.

We book the internal flights that we will require for our movements around Vietnam. Can Tho to Hoi An, and then Hoi An onto Hanoi. To get to Goa it looks like our cheapest option is to first make our way back to Bangkok (again!) and then our flight options become plentiful. After an afternoon of deliberation, weighing up the cost against long wait times between flights, our decision is made. Hanoi to Bangkok and then onto Goa via Kuala Lumpar in Malaysia; not the most direct route by any means, but cost friendly and with no seven hour waits between flights! The biggest plus is that we would be transit passengers in Kuala Lumpar rather than the alternative of having to negotiate the chaos of two Indian airports.

With our flights all arranged we start to make reservations for the hotels and guesthouses. Whilst the flights have no flexibility, we decide that it would be advantageous to allow ourselves more freedom with accommodation. With that in mind we make sure that all our bookings are refundable, in most cases up to twenty-four hours before our arrival date. The theory behind this is that it gives us more options on route to follow advice and tips from other travellers, we can then go 'off-piste' a little if we get the inclination. We go for the apartment option offered by Valerie in Goa, for one it is cheaper than guesthouses, but two it gives us cooking and washing facilities as well as not being confined to one solitary room for the two months plus!

September 2015

With all the fun of choosing, researching and booking the guesthouses and hotels finalised we move onto some of the less exciting necessities. We both require new passports; although they are not due to run out for another eighteen months or so, there are not enough blank pages left for the visas and stamps that we will require.

No sooner have the passports returned than we send them away again; first task is the visa required for Vietnam. This one is a quite an easy procedure – the ideal warm up for filling in the Indian visa application, they want to know everything about you, your parents, countries visited in the past, inside leg measurement (joking on that last one) …. Over the years we have been filling these forms in and they seem to get longer each year. If we had been going for our usual fortnight, we could have had an E-visa this year, but that is only valid for up to thirty days. As soon as the passport returns from the Vietnamese Embassy off it goes again to get the Indian visa. There is a huge sense of relief when the passports are back in our own hands, plenty of empty pages and the two visas that we require stamped in them. The visa for Thailand is automatically granted on arrival, or at least for the length of time that we are staying for. The Cambodia one can be arranged and paid for on arrival into the country.

We also need to sort out our home insurance for whilst we are away. Our policy lapses in December but because the house will be unoccupied for such a long time, we need to let them know. That is soon sorted and not too expensive either, the premium does go up a little for the time we are away and there is a couple of conditions that need to be met. We need to leave the central heating either on to reach a minimum temperature in the house or drain it completely. The second caveat is that the house must be checked by a responsible adult at least once a week, we already have that in hand.

It is all beginning to feel very real; one more turnover of the calendar and it will be there, albeit right towards the end of October. We are into the stage of counting in days now; our minds are whirring, still creating lists of things that need to be done nearer the time. Suddenly we have a glut of weekend activity, there is a birthday party, a retirement party plus a night out with some friends before we make our escape for the winter. Having something on the calendar most weekends does keep time moving fast – now all the planning is done we just want to go.

October 2015 – Countdown...

With one week to go excitement is building, I have a practise run at draining the central heating! The last-minute practicalities still to do; most preparing for worst case scenarios.

Currency wise we have some Thai Baht and American Dollars to collect. We only want a small amount of Thai money; enough to start us off as the exchange rate is extremely poor when getting it beforehand. American dollars we need as that is the only currency that you can use to pay for your Cambodian visa, plus American dollars are handy to have as they are universally accepted. We have already researched through Tripadvisor which banks we should use in each country to minimise ATM transaction charges, if all goes to plan we can avoid charges altogether, both from ATM and bank charges back home, there is nothing like making your money stretch that little bit further!

As well as sourcing the currency we also purchase five hundred pounds worth of Travellers Cheques, hopefully they will be coming on the whole journey and returning home with us – strictly for emergencies only. We already have a Western Union account, so I pass the details of that onto my sister, again just in case we have any disasters on route, bank cards all stolen etc. etc... We are not worried or expecting any of these worst-case scenarios – but it is still better to be prepared.

We have two folders full of flight bookings, reservations, insurance, passport and visa scans. Fail to prepare, prepare to fail!! Guide books are also packed; Alison always packs a spongebag full of tablets, hopefully covering all eventualities. We go on the theory working like an umbrella, if you carry it round all day, it does not rain. Packing is hard to plan, normally our cases weigh in at around the twelve-kilogram mark – or at least when we are heading out, coming back they are heavier due to the Old Monk Rum and Honeybee Brandy that we love. Cases get packed, unpacked, and then packed again repeatedly. It is difficult. We know that we need enough clothes for our first eleven days or so, then, once we get to our first stop in Cambodia we can get our laundry done. By the time we finish packing each case weighs around fourteen kilograms, heavier than what we would really like but manageable.

Tomorrow is the big day, my Dad is running us down to Peterborough station, it is an early start but setting the alarm clock on this occasion is a pleasure. Before we go to bed we attach the hose in readiness of draining the central heating first thing in the morning! We move all the cases downstairs, every preparation that we can think of has been made, and we have had long enough to plan - there is no excuse for any oversights! We are not sure how well we will sleep; it is always difficult when a big day is ahead, our minds are still doing mental gymnastics...

The Big Day Arrives...

28th October

We are awake early, 4 a.m. Far too early to get up so we roll over and try to get some more sleep. At 6:10 a.m. the phone rings, Waynes Dad letting us know that he will be around in half hour to pick us up for the train station. Were still in bed, whatever time we had told him we knew he would ring fifteen minutes before that! We get up, time for a quick breakfast, wash up the pots and then on with the last few jobs, drain the central heating, turn off the gas and switch off the water supply. Certain that everything is packed, all eventualities covered and nothing that we have forgotten the car is loaded up and we lock the door for what will be the last time for a few months.

The journey to Peterborough station goes quickly enough, we will get there before the main morning traffic hits. The weather is pouring down, it is quite amusing to us – another good reason to be leaving for warmer climes rather than a cold wet winter. Into Peterborough and a wrong turning just before the station, signposting is not that good and with the wipers going on fast easily missed. No problem as we are always arriving in plenty of time, that is a habit of ours, much sooner to be sat waiting than watching the clock and panicking! After quick goodbyes we check what platform our train leaves from before heading into the station café for a coffee to kill half hour or so.

The train arrives on time, our seats are reserved anyway, but the carriage was surprisingly empty. It was the first time since being together that we had ever used the train for a journey, a pleasant change from driving and very relaxing knowing that we have plenty of time. It continues to rain outside as we look through the windows, the highpoint of which was going past Arsenal's Emirates stadium.

After about an hour the train pulls into Kings Cross Station, a leisurely stroll with our luggage to get the tube to Heathrow. The tube journey is a little less comfortable than the first part, but all goes smoothly. It was the tube journey part that I was least looking forward to – so more relaxed now.

As usual we have arrived ridiculously early! Fortunately, the Qatar Airways desks are already open; no queues either, so we are quickly able to relieve ourselves of our hold luggage. We work our way through to the boarding gates, or at least the main halls as they are these days. Alison sets off the x-ray machines as usual with her bionic hip (replaced in 2005 but still going strong); this will no doubt be a recurring theme over the next few months! After a quick body scan, she is through, so we have a quick browse in all the shops that we cannot afford. We both phone home, let everyone know that we have arrived safely at the airport. To kill further time we have a couple of beers, begrudgingly paying the £4.35 a pint; the consolation being that we know we will be paying nothing like that for our upcoming ones for the next four months.

The first leg of our flight (Heathrow to Doha) is on time, this flight is on the Dreamliner, so plenty of legroom and spacious surroundings altogether, with the flight being very empty that just adds to the sense of comfort. We will not get bored for lack of choice on the entertainment system, hundreds of choices of films, documentaries, comedies, games etc. The music selection is even bigger and you can create your own playlists from all the albums that are available – definitely keep us occupied for the near seven-hour flight! The food is plentiful, almost too much, as we are not doing anything to create an appetite, strangely that does not stop the couple from behind us having a minor domestic before he asks for more, complaining the portion size wasn't big enough! Alison watches The Second Best Exotic Marigold Hotel film followed by some documentaries about Thai street food, getting the taste buds whetted for what is ahead of us. I snigger through three episodes of Moone Boy, I have watched them all before but they are hilariously funny.

With the clock going forward it is around midnight as we arrive in Doha, through the flight connection gates rather than arrivals. There is no time to spare as just the fifty-five minutes between our landing time and the next departure. It is good to stretch the legs though, knowing that we will soon be sat back down again – this time trying to get some sleep.

29th October

Doha is an amazing airport, vast, clean and with the biggest signage that we have ever seen. No problems in finding where we need to be, it is a strange experience here as there are lots of Arabs wandering around in the full white robes (Thobe or Thoub). No sooner do we find our gate and we are in the queue; a fast-moving one at that, and in no time at all we are in the departure pen awaiting boarding.

Upon getting onto the plane we are amazed by the sheer size, it is our first ever journey on an Airbus A380. Absolutely massive, a big wide stairway to the upper decks – not that we will be using them! Again, plenty of space and leg room – even for the likes of us in the cheap seats! Having expressed our joy at the comfort you would think it would be easy to sleep, but that is not the case. The flight is far busier for this leg of the journey, and the food just keeps on coming. How much can you eat when you are burning nothing off? On the plus side, each food visit does give a beer or wine opportunity, so not all bad...

We arrive in Bangkok on time, and promptly meet the first bottleneck of our journey; immigration. It takes around an hour to pass through here, on the plus side our hold luggage has already appeared on the carousel. Next mission is to find the airport station, in the past we have been on holiday and it would have been a taxi, thinking budget this time we start as we mean (and need) to go on. Armed with our BTS Skytrain map we head down into the bowels of the airport to await the shuttle that connects Bangkok's Suvarnabhumi Airport with the Skytrain. It is reassuringly secure; a couple of months ago there had been a bomb blast in Bangkok and since then security had been beefed up. As people exit the shuttle for the airport we are held back whilst the carriages are searched.

The first part is comfortable, the shuttle bus runs us to Phaya Thai which is on the BTS Sukhumvit line where we change our mode of travel. The stairs and our luggage are not compatible, a struggle commences as I start moaning that we have overpacked! Once we are aboard the Skytrain it fortunately runs right through to Asok station where we need to disembark. Again, more steps, but we soon navigate our way through the station and onto the streets into the heat, smells, and noise of Bangkok. With the Skytrain map put away, we dig out the next one – good old google maps. A short walk down Sukhumvit Road before turning off into Soi 23 to find our first hotel, the Admiral Premier Sukhumvit. This is from our original booking, when it was a brief holiday – so a little luxury to start with, in fact more than we planned as upon arrival we were upgraded to a suite; result!! The room is impressive, no chance of us using the kitchen and lounge facilities, we are planning to eat out at the street food stalls.

Bangkok

29th October

We stretch our legs and venture up to the roof top pool and that will about do us for the afternoon. Early evening and we head to the Soi Cowboy, just a five-minute walk from our hotel. It is a small lane but full of strip bars and drinking venues, we have a couple of beers before heading off on foot to Soi 38, a street famous for food stalls that we used last time we were here. Maybe our memories are deceiving us but it seems a lot smaller this time, less stalls? Some food stations are restaurant(ish), plastic chairs and wipeable tables but still an individual establishment, whilst others are more communal where you share a larger central seating area but get offered multiple menus from different vendors to choose from. We opt for a single stall (for ease) and go for a memorable dish from our last Thai holiday; green curry and at seventy baht (£1.25 in English), it is amazing - fresh, sharp, and aromatic – a perfect first meal. Rather than walk back we get on the Skytrain at Thong Lo, the station right by the end of Soi 38 and head back two stops to Asok and our hotel. 9 p.m. and we are done for!

30th October

Our first night in a strange bed and we sleep well, very well; a full twelve hours. By the time we were up showered and dressed the breakfast service was in full flow. Breakfasts on holiday are always a strange affair, it is as if they are trying to cater for every breakfast combination from around the globe – so it is never surprising that there always appears to be a mad option or two! Spaghetti anyone?

We start off with cereal, like ours at home, but with different branding. There is the bonus of proper orange juice and the coffee is superb, very strong. Seeing that it is our first breakfast away we feel obliged to go for the local option as our 'main', perhaps in a few weeks we will be craving the more familiar route! Alison opens with a fried rice dish whilst I go for the massaman curry – one of our favourite Thai meals, but must admit that we have never had it for breakfast before! All good so far - a solid eight out of ten. With there being no rush, we have another couple of coffees and browse the English print newspaper, it was quite amused to see the Andy Capp cartoon in the Bangkok Post – that brought back memories from years ago.

Whilst leaving the hotel later than planned, the entire day is still ahead of us. Within five minutes of walking we are back onto the main Sukhumvit road (which starts in Bangkok but runs for four hundred kilometres). It is then just a short walk to Asok station, where we purchase a one-day travel pass and with that full access to the city aboard the Skytrain. Today's plan is to visit Chinatown and do a self-guided walking tour from our guide book. The Skytrain is far busier than we remember it from our last visit, we change from the Sukhumvit line at Siam station onto the Silom line, where we are to get off at Saphan Taksin. Saphan Taksin is the last stop before crossing the river and is one of the main water taxi stops on the Chao Phraya River due to the proximity of the train links. We leave the station and head down towards the river, and after a five-minute wait we are on the water taxi heading along the river to the pier at Rachawong.

We soon find Chinatown and from that point there is a lot of confused map reading, one or two detours (another description of being lost), and pointing at our maps to friendly locals who are extremely helpful in keeping us (vaguely) heading in the right direction. Once we get to the food section there are lots of interesting sights... just not convinced how many of them that we would actually fancy eating though! The stand out memory was a flattened-out pigs' face that looked like it had been deep fried. As much as we both love the pig in all its eating forms, we are not sure about that!

Having completed our walking tour of Chinatown, and seen the main sights as per the guide book we take in a couple of firsts; Wat Pathum Khong Kha was a temple that we had never visited before and conveniently right on the doorstep of Chinatown. Access to it was a little strange, a short walk through a school playground so lots of smiles and hellos as we made our way. Swiftly following that we do our first market, Talat Kao; it is believed to be the oldest market in Bangkok and central to Chinatown delicacies - shark's fins, dried abalone (shellfish), fried puffed up fish stomachs and steamed bird's nests have earned it a reputation for catering to the more extreme end of Chinese cuisine. An inevitable first is also added to the list, Alison has the first blister! Fortunately, the walking for the day is about over, we retrace our routes and via the water taxi and Skytrain we head back to the sanctuary of our hotel and take the opportunity to catch some sun at the rooftop swimming pool. The pool is great, boasting an unobstructed view across the city skyline as the sun sets for the day.

Like last night we head to Soi 38 for our tea, looking forward to the pad thai that we remember – unfortunately on this occasion it does not live up to the memories; oh well! Because we still have our travel passes, we plan to head down to Patpong this evening. Patpong is world famous, a combination of markets, strip joints and at the heart of Bangkok's red-light district. The market is full of the usual mix of fakes; watches, Pandora bracelets, t-shirts, belts, handbags etc. We walk around the outside of the market and get various offers of shows, the most regular one involving ping pong balls! We get the odd glimpse of what goes on inside these places through the curtained doors as they try to tempt you inside – we decide not to partake. We leave here and head back towards our hotel, via one beer down the Soi Cowboy at a bar called Tilac – unfortunately tonight we have missed happy hour.

31st October

Woke up late again, the bed is comfortable and the duvet so soft. Quick showers and then we head down for breakfast. I must still be half asleep as I put tom yum goong soup onto a plate – much to Alisons amusement! Just to add to my embarrassment I then get a mouthful of lemongrass, grimacing and pulling faces as it is very fragrant to say the least. Luckily, I manage to take the taste away with plenty of black coffee and cakes – we are loving these breakfasts but carry on like this and we will be carrying suitcases full of clothes that are a size too small.

Breakfasts completed and we make our way to Asok station to catch the Skytrain, heading down to the river again. It is a slightly longer river journey than yesterdays, three piers further on to Tha Tien, opposite the fantastic Wat Arun temple. We smile to ourselves as Wat Arun is surrounded by scaffolding; not sure if it is just us, but over the years we have seen a lot of scaffolding which ruins so many photograph opportunities. We are not too worried as we have seen it in full glory on our previous Thailand visit. We take the little river crossing ferry nonetheless and wander around the temple grounds and gardens, this is well worth doing as they are stunning and so well kept. We enter the inner temple and witness a monk giving an audience.

After making our way back across the river we wait for another river taxi, this time getting off at Phra Arthit pier. We take a wander around the Phra Sumen Fort on the waterfront, spotting a large water monitor (lizard type thing). With numerous purchases of bottled water on route we make our way to Khao San road, backpackers heaven. There are numerous travel agencies down here selling all kinds of excursions, including buses to Siem Reap at a fraction of our air fare, too late; our flights are already booked and paid for. There is a market down the centre of Khao San road selling lots of cheap clothes and the usual tat! Beer was on the more expensive side down here, but that was not going to stop us enjoying an ice cold one. We find a small bar with an even smaller dog (Alison says cute); beer excellent, a chilled glass straight from the freezer is simply perfect on hot days. We decide that we may return to Khao San road to do some shopping when we are on our quick stopover as we head to India.

Retracing our steps we catch the river taxi again, this time heading back towards home, but getting off at Pak Khlong Talat to visit the flower market of the same name. It's a bit late in the day (afternoon by now), so a lot of the hustle and bustle has already finished. It is still a worthwhile visit, very interesting. As well as all the ladies making garlands and floral tributes there are stalls that are selling chillies, onions and garlic by the lorry load – a very fragrant and pleasant smell throughout the place. We both pop to the toilets in the retail area of the flower market and Alison is surprised to see a urinal in the ladies' toilets, obviously catering for the transgender society of Bangkok!

We decide that it is time for us to head back down the river and catch the Skytrain and return to base, it will give us time for another early evening swim before we head out again. All this tramping around streets in the heat and in flip-flops is hard work! We have a leisurely swim, more a cooling dip and use of the sunbeds rather than anything energetic, before heading back to our room for our showers.

Alison causes chaos at Asok station; she tried using yesterday's day pass rather than todays, fortunately a helpful security man is on hand and scans us through the gates. With that in mind we decide it will be best that we bin the Skytrain passes at the end of each day, rather than putting them on the bedside cabinet as they all look identical! Once safely through the gates we head to Soi 38 again. This time we choose a more communal stall area, no sooner have we got sat down and menus start being thrust at us! Having chosen from the menu we most fancied we go for a curry soup with noodles and a bottle of Chang to wash it down with; fantastic meal, a solid nine out of ten.

By the time we have finished we are still in good time for the happy hour(s) at the Soi Cowboy strip of bars, a perfect way to end the day – time to relax and just watch the world go by. There are lots of semi-naked ladies, some that might have more than you bargained for; but guess that is some people's thing? Must admit some are very shapely and attractive and very, very convincing! Tonight there is a lot of fancy dress going on, Halloween. We think there must also be a high turnover of girls in the job market, some of the matching ensemble of shoes and underwear with sparkly belts seem less than an ideal fit!! There is a really good atmosphere about the place, pretty girls, people watching and live football being shown on the screens all readily available.

Alison is concerned about the health of some of the older men who are heading into the 'inner sanctum' of some of these establishments, would they ever be seen alive again? If not, guess that is the way to go with a huge great smile on your face! Having had a beer with our meal and a couple more at Tilac's. I have the need for the toilet, so must make my way inside... The best way I can describe inside is that it is like walking into a bar but on that bar is a whole selection of semi-naked ladies auditioning for a Robert Palmer music video, (think Addicted to Love). Luckily, I can see where the toilets are so head straight there. Much to my amusement there is a viewing pane, a bit like looking through a letterbox, so that whilst you release the beer you do not miss any of the show, of course I was more interested in the football...

After another beer we settle our bill and head back to the hotel. Alison decides that popping her blisters is the best option, hopeful that will speed up the healing process. The alarm clock is being set tonight as tomorrow we are on the move, a flight to Chiang Mai awaits us. As much as we love Bangkok three days at a time is plenty, we are very much looking forward to the change of location and hopefully a slower pace of life for the next five days.

Chiang Mai & Chiang Rai

1st November

Today is our last breakfast at the Admiral Premier Sukhumvit; excellent as usual. Rather than taking our entire luggage with us we opt to leave two bags in storage at the hotel here, it will make for an easier journey to the airport!

We fly to Chiang Mai from Suvarnabhumi Airport, the same one that we arrived here from, so today it is the reverse journey, BTS Skytrain to the Airport Rail Link. Having managed this once before with all our luggage it should be a doddle this time, we are both gaining confidence in our ability to get around using public transport; previous holidays had always been with transfers included, or if having organised themselves and not being on a budget, by using taxis.

The journey to the airport goes smooth (as usual we are there in plenty of time). There was one comedy moment at Asok Skytrain station as man and luggage were separated at the ticket barrier, best described as like a magician's assistant being cut in half! If you have luggage you have to use the gate and let a ticket officer let you through, auto-barriers are so sensitive that you cannot get away dragging (or pushing) your luggage. The airport check in all runs smoothly and it is always reassuring when you see that your flight is running on time.

Our flight with Thai Airways is reasonable, and although a short flight (one hour ten minutes) we do get fed. Before long we take off and no sooner are we up in the air being served with a snack box, containing a couple of finger sandwiches. Strangely the lady sat next to me makes a double-decker out of the two and eats all in one go! In the snack box there is also a sweet treat in the shape of the Thai Airways emblem, I think it is a cake and try to take a bite from it much to

Alison's amusement. It is a plastic case, with the treat inside! Obviously, it is one of those days for comedy.

We swiftly arrive in Chiang Mai, and with it being a domestic flight we are soon out the other side of the airport and into a taxi. It is a short and cheap taxi ride to our second hotel stroke hostel – SK House 2. Check in is a swift affair and we are shown to our clean but basic room that will be our home for the next five nights. Our initial impressions are good; basic but functional, breakfast is not included but there is a restaurant area downstairs if we decide to eat in.

With our minimal luggage hardly being worthy of unpacking we head straight back downstairs, looking to venture out and get our bearings of Chiang Mai before darkness. Before we can get through the reception we are intercepted by Tony, the rotund proprietor of the hotel. Tony swiftly turns on his salesman patter and tries to sell us various excursions, and although we are planning to book the odd day out, we want to wander around and check the going rate of trips before committing to anything. For the two trips that we are interested in Tony wants six thousand baht in total.

Having successfully fended off Tony's hard sell we do get out to explore - and almost immediately get lost. There is only one such thing to be done in this kind of crisis; drink beer. Stopping for a beer was a stroke of genius, without knowing where you are a map is next to useless, fortunately for us a man in the bar sees our predicament, knew what street we are on and set us in the right direction. We head back to base, better prepared now for finding our way back out tonight in the dark.

Sunday in Chiang Mai is the big night of the week, market night. With that in mind we have a quick shower, change of clothes and head back out again – map firmly in hand. We find our way to where we need to be, Sunday Walking Street; it is heaving! Stall after stall of amazing food, some that we do recognise and others that no way in the world would we consider eating! With all these options we decide that dinner will be a mobile affair tonight, so with a starter of squid tentacles on a stick with a spicy sauce accompaniment we start our food extravaganza. The squid is followed by quail egg wontons and stuffed pancakes, all delicious. We find a bar and have a beer or two to wash dinner down and people watch before returning to the market. There is a lot to see and buy but we are aware of how long we are away for; damage would be likely, as well as giving us even more to carry around for the next four months or so.

Upon arriving back at SK House 2 we are again accosted by Tony, and with being a bit more informed on the prices of excursions we manage to barter him down to five thousand baht for the two excursions! We head up to our room, an exceptionally large bed which is very comfortable and a wall mounted rotating fan – what more could be required (or expected) for the price of accommodation here.

2nd November

We both slept very well, the room was fine – not too hot. With no breakfast included we head out to the bar (The European) where we had got lost at yesterday; as well as serving beer and directions there was also a breakfast menu! Following our 'local' breakfasts of the last few days in Bangkok we opt for the full English, and to be fair it was a decent attempt. With a couple of coffees inside us we are now fully awake and alert, ready to explore Chiang Mai and its hundreds of temples – and that is not an exaggeration.

Having left the European we decide to follow the walking tour as set out in our guidebook, and promptly realise that we have been walking in the wrong direction! Fortunately getting lost on a regular basis is not an issue as time is on our side, and you often discover something that you would not have done otherwise (glass half full shining through!).

The temples are stunning, glittering in the sunlight against a backdrop of a perfect blue sky and mountains all around. Luckily, we are both wearing sandals / flip-flops as shoes are on and off every five minutes or so as you enter a different temple or part of another temple in the same complex. Alison, in full charge of the guidebook, instructs me to take photographs of an old gum tree – to be fair it is quite an impressive gum tree. We wander further around the complex before coming across a sign in front of another gum tree – the real one, the important one that the guidebook is referring to. Avoiding confusion, we delete the photos of the first gum tree and take a couple of shots of the correct one (although they do look identical).

With the sun beating down we have already ticked off several of the key Temples, Wat Chiang Man, the Megrai Shrine, the Three Kings Monument, Wat Chedi Luang and Wat Phra Singh (one of the oldest temples and visible from our hotel). We decide that with the heat and all of the walking that we have already done to head back to base, via a very rustic bar. An ice-cold beer has rarely tasted better and it turns out to be a great stop as we get chatting to some of the locals.

Back at the hotel we find Tony and pay for our excursions, so tomorrow will bring us the highlights of Chiang Mai, followed the next day with a trip to Chiang Rai. Now a dip in the pool beckons, it is only a small pool with no sunbeds to read or relax in but it is so refreshing after a sweltering day traipsing around Chiang Mai city.

After a spell of relaxation and reading in our room we get showered, changed and ready to go out again. Tonight we have a second walking tour, again from the guidebook - this time in the direction of the night bazaar. We find Somphet market and decide that it is time to eat, tonight's food is chicken chilli and chicken garlic, both particularly good. With our stomachs full we head down Tha Phae Road where we revisit a couple of wats (temples). The night bazaar market is much the same as last night's Sunday market, stalls selling pretty much the same local goods. We head back into the centre of the city along Walking Street, a whole lot quieter tonight, but we visit the same bar as it has good Wi-Fi to contact home and decent music.

Having had a beer (or two), and with emails sent we head back towards the hotel, only to find a corner of the city that is very lively, so we stop for another drink. We have discovered the area where all the youngsters hang out, the music is a little louder here, still good though and a suitable place to people watch. What is certain though, we are upping the average age, but there are a few other 'oldies' around here as well! We will have to visit here again, another night when we do not need to be up quite so early. Home to bed!

3rd November

With a seven thirty pick up for our excursion to Chiang Mai National Park we only have time for a coffee and a round of toast this morning, very disappointing compared to the standard of breakfasts that we have been enjoying since our travels began!

Our collection is on time, a small minibus containing eleven of us of various nationalities. We soon leave the city of Chiang Mai and are heading towards one of the largest waterfalls in the Chom Thong district - our first stop, Wachirathan Falls - which translates as Diamond Creek Falls. It is very impressive but also very damp as a constant mist seems to be spraying from it in our directions. We are still able to dry off the camera and get some decent photos of it!

Photos taken and our small group are all loaded back onto the bus for a visit to a small Karen (indigenous people) village. At these types of places, you are always suspicious that they are set up purely for the tourist hordes but even if they are you do get an idea of how they live. This one was a settlement of about a dozen wooden houses, all on raised stilts, set with a large paddy field behind them all. They are very self-sufficient judging by the number of chickens wandering around, we guess they are for both their eggs and the cooking pot? There were also many puppies, hopefully they were just for pets, some were so small that they can only have been a matter of days old. Our group was given a demonstration of how they produce woven shawls and bedding, very clever as they do it sat down using long looms. The products that they sell take from four days to one month to produce, no doubt depending on factors such as the size and level of intricacy involved. They are very impressive and colourful, but like so much of what you find on your travels – what would you do with it once back home? They are all traditional designs and made of various materials, cotton, hemp and then embroidered; fortunately for us there is no sales pitch which is a pleasant surprise. We browse the racks of completed items and then head back outside to the village.

With everyone back aboard we head off to our second waterfall of the day; Sirithan waterfall. By this point we are now in the Doi Inthanon National Park and having been spoilt by the first waterfall we are not as impressed with this one! It is amazing how quickly you get blasé about some of the amazing scenery and experiences, if we had been shown this one first then we would have been more excited. Searching Wikipedia for more facts about it justifies our minds – it does not even have an entry! Our watches (and stomachs) confirm that we are halfway through the day, so time for the obligatory market followed by lunch. Lunch turns out to be a very tasty affair with lots of choice, overly impressed as previous experience and memories suggests that they can be very hit and miss! Over food we get chatting to three fellow travellers from London who are on our minibus, they are travelling onto Laos, Vietnam and India, a similar path to us.

Once fed and watered it is back onto what is the increasingly uncomfortable minibus, our next destination being the highest point in Thailand. After a further hour's travel, we arrive; Doi Inthanon, 2565 metres high and a very cool fourteen degrees! The surroundings are quite surreal, best described as rain forest, there is a damp misty feel, and most surfaces are covered with a green moss. Although it is obviously always damp and misty up here, we do have the added 'bonus' of a touch of rain – and for the first time in a week we feel cold. Amongst all the greenness, from both the plant canopy and the moss that has enveloped anything made of stone there are some very colourful birds, the red ones are just so bright (almost neon), but also super elusive whenever a camera is pointed in their direction.

Our final stop of the day is at the nearby pagodas dedicated to the King and Queen of Thailand. These are so high up that when you look down you are peering through low-lying clouds. Today we can declare as a keep-fit day, so many steps that we have climbed. The gardens here are perfectly manicured and very impressive; unfortunately the backdrop is just grey and cloudy. These two chedi's (stupa style temples) were built by the Thai Air force to honour the sixtieth birthday of King Bhumibol Adulyadej in 1987, and the sixtieth birthday anniversary of Queen Sirikit in 1992, respectively.

All that is left of our day is the long journey home. Falling asleep so that the time passes quickly would be the best option and also reduce the scare factor - lunatic drivers mean that Thailand ranks at number four for road deaths in the world. Amazingly we both manage to do that; we can only put it down to the bumpy road rocking us to sleep as most unusual that we sleep whilst travelling.

It is nice to get back to our hotel, the usual pattern though – just enough time for a quick shower, change of clothes and we are back out again. It is a leisurely walk to a local bar where we get chatting to a medical student who is keen to show us photos of what seems like his entire family on his mobile phone! With polite goodbyes we head to the Bamboo Café for dinner where tonights meals of choice are the penang curry and khao soi (curry noodles originating from Burma). The standard of food once again can only be described as amazing, with their use of spices they make English food appear so dull and plain.

Tonight, unusually, we are too full for more beer, though with it still being relatively early we do stop for one in a quiet bar near to Zoe's Corner. It kills an hour with a combination of people watching and flicking through the photos that we have taken so far on our travels. Having settled our bar tab we have a leisurely stroll home, once again there is an alarm set for in the morning – Chiang Rai beckons.

4th November

Our alarm wakes us from our sleeps at 6:45 a.m. Again, only time for a disappointing breakfast of coffee and toast before our early pick-up.

As yesterday, our transport was bang on time, but today we have the added advantage of being first on the minibus – hopefully we have made a wise choice of seats! It is not long before our unintended tour of Chaing Mai city is complete and all our fellow tourists have been collected. Today we have an even smaller number, just the nine of us plus our very cheerful guide Pia.

It takes us one hour to get to our first stop, it is some hot stinky springs where the locals are doing a good trade in selling eggs that can then be boiled in the spring water. The smell is one of sulphur, so not that pleasant but still quite impressive how these springs that are running through what has turned into a tourist spot / car park can cook your egg for breakfast.

Back onto the minibus and a further one hour plus where we arrive at the White Temple (or Wat Rong Khun to give it its proper name). On first sight it is very impressive, it almost looks like it is a carving made from ice, then the closer you get the more bizarre it appears. The main approach is up via a type of catwalk that has a moat with hundreds of hands reaching upwards, some with painted nails, others holding skulls. Once you get into the main temple it is far more contemporary, a nice mix of modern and traditional, none of the bizarre items from outside have made it into here. The whitewash and mirrors further complement the 'ice' look. Further around the temple complex we come across pathways where the whole roof structure above is made of thousands of little charm necklaces. Every turn and there would be something else that caught your eye, no doubt you could visit a second time and notice something that you had missed before.

Even the visit to the toilets were interesting, rather than the usual Gents or Ladies signs there were grotesque figures outside each of the two door options, it was obvious which door was which as these figures had full genitalia on show, and if that was not graphic enough there was a Mr. Whippy style poo behind them, obviously for anyone who had not worked out that these were indeed the toilets! We could not help but imagine what was going on in the mind of the designer / architect of this place – amazing, beautiful, interesting but also odd. Apparently, it is still work in progress, so there is no telling what he will produce next?

With the help of Wikipedia, we were able to throw more light on this amazing place, firstly it is not due to be completed until the year 2070....so I would love to see it in its full glory while celebrating my hundredth birthday, though we may well be long gone by then! It is a local artist, Chalermchai Kositpipat, who is behind the structure, as a temple to Lord Buddha he believes that it will help him achieve eternal life. As mentioned earlier, it is very traditional in places but outside there are influences of Western culture, including Michael Jackson, Harry Potter, Hello Kitty, Freddy Kruger, Superman, and the Terminator. Complete madness!!

With our time up here it is back to the bus, but first, on the advice of Pia we buy some small juicy pineapple from one of the market vendors in the car park. It was one of the sweetest and succulent pineapple that we have ever tasted – luckily Alison always carries tissues and wipes so we can get the stickiness off our hands!

It is another hours' drive before we reach the area known as the Golden Triangle, this was an old trading area between Thailand, Laos, and Myanmar (or Burma in those days). The gold that is being referred to is opium, or black gold as it was known. Before boarding the tourist boat, we hand over our passports as we are making a short journey across the Mekong River into Laos, but before disembarking we sail up the river to where it all opens out and you can see Myanmar. Hence the name the Golden Triangle!

We disembark in Laos, all very disappointing – this location must be there purely for the tourists getting off the boat, fake handbags, leather belts, whiskeys infused with various animals (or animal parts). The guy is offering tastings of various whiskeys, no doubt to create sales, so, even though we do not like whiskey we give it a go. Alison tries the snake option whilst I taste the whiskey with the marinated tiger penis! Additional options included scorpion, turtle and gecko. Although our 'experience' of Laos can only be described as manufactured there are stunning views across the Mekong as we look back towards Thailand and further down the river towards Myanmar.

Following the short journey across the river we are reunited with our passports and it is a twenty-minute drive to where lunch will be served. The buffet style lunch was not a patch on yesterdays but we did get to try mango sticky rice and bananas in coconut milk; our fruit intake is on the up.

Back on board the minibus and a short ride to see the border crossing with Myanmar (we are now at the most northern point of Thailand). There is not a huge amount to see, it mainly consists of a fifty or so metre long bridge where the time zone changes by thirty minutes, and just for good measure you also have to switch the side of the road that you drive on! Having spent a quarter of an hour or so watching cars criss-cross each other to get to the correct side of the road it is time to return to the bus.

It is a longer journey this time before we reach our next stop. The tribal village of Akha and the Kayan people; the Akha are originally of Chinese descent and there are around eighty thousand of them living in the north of Thailand, primarily in Chiang Rai. The Kayan people were originally from Burma, what these days we call Myanmar, and are often referred to as the Long Neck Karen people.

Whilst the Akhan have been accepted and are supported by the Thai government the Karen people are still self-supporting and have no legal recognition in Thailand in regards to voting, healthcare and such. There are around six and a half thousand of these people, spread out across three areas of Thailand. To create the long neck they apply neck rings from an early age (normally around the five-year mark), and keep increasing the number of these rings until the age of forty-five. The total weight can often reach five kilograms or more, and they can never be taken off as the neck muscle would be too weak. Even though they are not officially recognised the children do have the option of attending school.

With this being the final stop of our excursion, it is time for the long journey home, it has been a good trip with a good mix of people, alongside us there were three more Brits, a couple of Europeans and a couple of Americans. The American couple were very friendly and called us cool for what we are doing! Once again, we are the oldest on the bus. We did not manage to sleep on this journey; it was very twisting and turning as well as being very windy. At one point there were road signs suggesting 'low gear' and '40kmh', our driver did brake down from the hundred he was doing down to eighty. The driver Mr. San and Pia never stopped chatting for the whole three-hour journey! Pia is the best tour guide that we have had so far, ridiculously cheerful but with a top that had detachable sleeves which she could take off or put back on as required. Definite Dragons Den idea there; so versatile!

Tonight is our quickest shower and change of clothing yet, it was well past our tea-time by the time we were returned to our hotel. We have a quick bite to eat, and Alison points out at 11:20 p.m. that she has technically gone twenty-four hours without a drink (conveniently forgetting the snake whiskey tot). We find a bar with live music; the band is good but then finish about three songs later, just after we get sat down. Knowing that we have no alarm clock in the morning we are not yet ready for home so visit the quiet bar on Zoe's corner. What we notice tonight is that the youngsters (compared to us) pop into the cheap bar to get their 'bucket' filled before going back outside to drink in the street where the overflow from Zoe's in Yellow (full name) all congregate. It is heaving tonight, but as soon as midnight strikes all the shutters come down and everyone heads home. It is the first night where we have seen midnight!

5th November

For some reason we always sleep better when we know there is no alarm clock, and of course the drink may have helped! With a leisurely day planned there is no need to rush about, so we head off into Chiang Mai city for another 'full English' at the European.

Having filled our stomachs and livened ourselves up with coffee we head to the Thaphae Gate entrance into the city and down the road of the same name to see the two temples that we missed the other day. One was really impressive, all made of teak, although the best angles for pictures was thwarted by a persistent, annoying taxi driver trying to sell us excursions we were not interested in. The second temple was nothing that we had not seen before, although fortunately for Alison it did have toilet facilities as she was suddenly caught unaware! With that potential disaster averted the most memorable part was that it must have been on the itinerary of a Japanese tour group, tuk-tuk after tuk-tuk turned into the grounds as we were leaving.

Following our guidebook, we head down some of the old streets selling gold, silver and leather, lots of bling, before making our way to a temple we had previously visited where you could chat with the resident monks. We sat with a young monk who gave us an interesting insight into Buddhism and his daily life, it is a considerably basic existence going back hundreds of years, yet they all have mobile phones and iPads. We pick up a leaflet from him to learn more.

With the heat beating down we head for the shade under a tree and a browse of our leaflet, where we are approached by three Thai students; they ask if they can interview us as part of their English language assignment, that is not a problem at all. After two failed attempts due to equipment problems, we take part in a rather stilted interview, answering some of the questions for the third time! With a few language difficulties it is all caught on camera ready to be sent to their teacher for assessment. We were surprised to find that they were all nineteen years old, they would easily have passed for fifteen.

On with our travels and a search for an internet café, (we need to get a document signed, scanned and emailed back home). With this mission accomplished we decide to head back to the hotel but via a restaurant recommendation from a French guy we had got talking to earlier. He had assumed we were lost (not on this occasion), but after a brief chat he tipped us off about a Burmese restaurant called The Swan. We check the menu and decide that is tonight's destination of choice.

By 3 p.m. we are back at the hotel where we discover that there is a roof-top sun terrace, so decide to get our books and have a read and relax. The only downside is that there is cage after cage of wild birds, we would love to set them all free! Having rested we head to the room, get showered and head out for the evening.

On our way to The Swan we stop off at another one of our regular café bars, the Bamboo Café and have a banana milkshake; excellent, very thick and creamy, if only we had discovered it sooner! We get chatting to the man who gave us directions on our very first day earlier in the week; he is living here on a fact-finding mission for his planned retirement next year. As much as we are envious of him, he is of us and our plans for our travels right into March next year. The French guy was correct, a great recommendation and we can now add Burmese food to our list of meals, both the chicken curry and noodle dish were tasty, superb food and the best lime sodas too.

We head back towards the hotel, another drink in the Bamboo Café, Chang beer though this time, before heading nearer to home and our regular stop in the quiet bar on Zoe's Corner. We get chatting to a street seller who is trading in woven bracelets, her English is excellent; she follows the tourist routes selling to try and earn some money to send back home. She likes the tourist resort of Phuket best but comes back to Chiang Mai as this is where her family are, two children of nine and thirteen. Once again, the clock has reached midnight and the shutters are being pulled down. Not bad for two oldies drinking until closing time!

Back to Bangkok

6th November

It is back to Bangkok for us today, we try a new café for breakfast, closer to the hotel. Alison has a bit of an iffy stomach today so opts for the fruit salad and yoghurt; it is massive, bananas, mango, melon, apple and pineapple! - absolutely delicious and for just fifty baht, although the accompanying coffee could have been better. I choose the omelette, again very good, before helping Alison wade through hers.

We check out of the hotel by nine thirty and hail a local taxi (songthaew), which is best described as a truck with no doors or windows and a row of seats facing each other along each side. Luggage loaded and it is just a ten-minute journey to the airport. At the airport Alison fills in this diary with a footnote of 'wildlife' seen in Chiang Mai, rats both dead and alive, scorpion (dead), squirrels and various things we would not consider eating impaled on sticks!

The flight all runs smooth, just a delay of fifteen minutes to the scheduled time, and with it being a domestic flight we are very quick in getting through and out of the airport on our arrival back in Bangkok. Using the same route as our arrival last time (only with a lot less luggage), we make our way to our next hotel using the Air Rail Link and the Skytrain. Our plan is to get checked into our new digs, the Amora Neoluxe before heading back to the Admiral Premier and reclaim the other half of our luggage. The first impressions of the Amora Neoluxe are all good, although we do have problems locating the light switches. Alison eventually discovers that she holds all the power as everything is controlled by a snazzy touchpad her side of the bed. It is a large room, big TV, but with only one English language channel – a news channel, but strangely even that is transmitted by

France 24. The lack of TV channels was more than made up for with a massive bath, it was huge; a proper lay down and relax job!

As it has been a day of sitting around, we decide to walk to Soi 38 for our evening meal even though it is still very warm. Crispy pork noodles and rice are the mains we opt for, sold to us by a persistent elderly man. It is, once again, an excellent choice, very tasty and the crisp pork especially delicious. With our meal finished we catch the Skytrain from Thong Lo back towards Asok, the Soi Cowboy and our hotel.

As we approach the Tilac bar we are initially shown into the 'inner sanctum', we quickly retreat to the seating outside and people watching; it seems busy tonight. The four Americans at the table next to use are impressed by the whiskey prices, so after drinking plenty of them they are soon moved to a more coveted central table where massages ensued. I was offered a massage but declined, must add that mine was offered by the ageing bar staff rather than the nubile young ladies! Two lads next to us were enticed inside by a pair of extremely attractive young ladies; they might well end up with a higher bar bill than originally planned! We head back to the room as neither feeling one hundred percent, an early night will do us good.

7th November

It is not a good night's sleep, while I am not too bad, Alison is still feeling ropey. Breakfast is attended though, and it is a broad selection complete with a proper toaster. We are fed up of those conveyer belt types that gives you the choice of either warm bread after one circuit, or set the smoke alarms off after two. I am slightly put off as the plates are square, one of my real pet-hates, but the omelette (round) is about making up for it.

With both of us under the weather we opt for a day around the pool, remaining near to the toilets and the comfort of our room, just in case. The weather is overcast, but still very warm, so the roof top pool with its nice decking and comfortable sun-loungers will suit us nicely. Rain had been forecast but we only got a handful of spots. I make a short trip to the nearest 7 – 11 supermarket for some crisps and cans of Coca Cola as we begin to perk up.

Feeling better by mid-afternoon we decide to have a walk around the park on Sukhumvit Road. It is a pleasant park full of pigeons, enthusiastic youngsters playing every sport and joggers (far too hot for any of that). There is also a lake in the middle with lots of terrapins. We walk to find the Rembrandt hotel where we stayed on our first visit to Bangkok, it looks just as we remembered it! Wandering back home, we discuss what is for tonights tea as Alison not certain what she fancies. Looking at our watches we wait outside the 7 – 11 supermarket, for the clock to reach 5 p.m. - they lock the beer fridges up at certain times of the day here – proper licensed drinking hours when purchasing in a shop.

After returning to our room and running another massive bath we get changed and head out for food….to the local Subway restaurant; the foods not bad there either. Seeing rats wandering the street we head to the Lighthouse Bar; the staff are younger and more attractive here. Glimpsing inside the podium dancers are barely moving, then the music gets more up tempo and they are off! I am trying to convince Alison that she should get some sparkly studded pants like they all wear here. It is another early night for us, still a little below par but confident that tomorrow we will be back to normal service.

8th November

Today is our last full day in Bangkok, and Alison is feeling a whole lot better. As per Tripadvisor tips she opts for a yoghurt option for breakfast, me omelette (again) with salad!?!

Via the Skytrain we head off to the Chatuchak weekend market; the largest in the whole of Thailand. It is mostly undercover and row upon row of stalls, some selling the usual tourist tat, but others live animals, from squirrels wearing hats to puppies! We found a map detailing the layout but that did not help much – you need to be a dedicated shopper to persevere here, although it is worth the visit just to experience the scale and the bizarre sights. Forty minutes was plenty for us!

We have a quick look around the adjacent park before heading back aboard the BTS (where I do my good deed for the day in giving BTS Skytrain guidance to another foreign tourist; obviously look like I know what I am doing), and on to Lumphini Park. It seems odd that there can be such a huge green space right in the heart of the city, there is a large lake, cycle lanes, joggers and lots of Tai Chi going on, mostly by older people but with a large sword involved. With some good pictures of a water monitor and egret we head back to the air-conditioned BTS, so pleasant in the heat of the day.

We get off the Skytrain again just to take some pictures of the Royal Sporting Club of Bangkok, this consists of a horse racing course around the outside with a golf course in the centre, you could start a new type of biathlon here? Back aboard the Skytrain and a revisit of Jim Thompsons house, we have been once before and remember it as being a cool oasis – let us hope our memories are correct!

Our memories have served us well, it is a beautiful wooden house that belonged to Jim Thompson, the silk-man who mysteriously disappeared whilst travelling and was never seen again. The house that he built along with the grounds are all in the care of the Jim Thompson Foundation, along with his art collection. There is also a detailed and interesting explanation of how silk comes to be. During our tour Alison feels a bit faint, so the tour guide provides her with some water; obviously this house does not agree with her as she was not great on our last visit here either!

It is late afternoon so we head back to the hotel, and we decide that we will return to this hotel when we pop back to Bangkok early January before we head off to India. It has a nice pool and serves good breakfasts, plus we have also collected enough free night's courtesy of Hotels.com to cover our two-night stay. We head up to the pool where it is a lot busier today, we think that by this time of day the heat has beaten everyone and the temptation of the pool wins.

It is our last visit to Soi 38 for some time tonight, Alison fancies a green curry while I plan one last massaman. Mine is delivered and eaten before Alison's appears, it is due to their way of eating, all meals are for sharing. Starters and mains can roll out together, and not always in that order! The consolation to this is that you do end up sharing meals, and therefore get to try more... and the wait is always worthwhile!

Final visit to the Soi Cowboy, I have a beer, Alison a water. Aston Villa v Manchester City on the giant TV. It is just the one drink before we head back to the room and game three of our self-titled Scrabble World Series. Alison is left kicking herself as she missed out on a good finish still to lose by four points. On the move again tomorrow; next stop Cambodia!

Top row: Dancers at the Erawan Shrine, Bangkok. Zoe In Yellow and Wat Mahawan, Chiang Mai

Middle: Long Necked Karen and Wat Rong Khun (White Temple), Chiang Rai

Bottom: Three Kings Monument, Chiang Mai, Ordination Hall, Wat Arun & Chao Phraya River, Bangkok

Siem Reap, Cambodia

9th November

Alison is feeling tip-top today, thank goodness, so tucks into her omelette with gusto. I have omelette plus eggy bread, samosas and salad – being on holiday all rules are thrown out of the window.

We head back to our room, round up the last of our belongings and well ahead of schedule we start our journey to the airport. It is a different airport today, Don Mueang, but we are by now confident in our ability of negotiating the public transport systems. BTS Skytrain ticket in hand, cursing all our luggage we make our way to Mo Chit where we need to catch the A1 bus to the airport. Lots of steps on route but aside from that everything runs smoothly.

Its only eleven o' clock when we arrive and we are unable to check in until 11:50 a.m., so more time waiting and people watching; there is some strange attire being worn for travelling! Unusually Alison gets through the scanners without bleeping, but we do notice how many people are pulled up for liquids in their hand luggage, it has only been fourteen years since the rule has been in place! Knowing that we are getting no food on the flight we opt for some sandwiches and ice-cream sundaes, both the strawberry and chocolate were delicious. Sat waiting for our flight we wish we were flying with Nokair, their plane looks like a giant bird, the plane nose is painted as a beak and they have a cartoon ducks head as an emblem which is emblazoned on the tail fin.

We are soon aboard our flight; it is busy and on time. We do not seem to be up in the air for any length of time, just long enough to fill in the visa on arrival forms. It took us longer to get from our hotel to the airport this morning than what our flight, Bangkok to Siem Reap takes!

The Cambodia visa process is very slick, you hand in your completed form, passport photo (one we prepared earlier), passport and the money in American dollars at one end of the counter and collect five minutes later from the other end. Passport control is also a new experience, as well as the traditional glance at the passport photo and then looking us up and down, our fingerprints are also taken digitally. With our baggage collected and tuk-tuk secured we head off to the Yellow Hostel; not convinced our driver knew where it was but he asks fellow drivers and we are on our way – in the rain!

We pull up outside the Yellow Hostel, pay our driver and he tries to sell us his excursion for Angkor Wat, we take his name and number. It is a warm welcome from reception along with the news that their driver is waiting for us at the airport – a pick-up was included in our hotel booking but we had never received their reply to confirm it was happening. Apologies all round! Room 106 is our base for the next eight days, basic to say the least, it is clean though and the wardrobe is just a hook on the wall. Also on the walls and doors are signs saying no guns, no drugs and no durians are allowed inside the hostel. The bathroom, sink and toilet are in the wet room style. Exploring outside there is a nice pool area with some chairs to relax in too.

It is not going to be long before its dark so we venture out, not sure of where we are and where we want to be going! We find nothing so head back to the hotel, buy a beer each and get a map from reception, plus advice... a tuk-tuk to Pub Street is one American dollar. We also find out that the hotel does the Angkor Wat tour for fifteen dollars, that is five less than the guy who brought us from the airport. We go to the pool area to drink our beers but are soon driven back by the mosquitos, so we head upstairs to our room.

Alison always heads to test the showers out first, partly because I am as blind as a bat once I take my glasses off, but having tried every combination of taps she is unable to get a drop of water. I pop down to reception for assistance. Within minutes a man pops up and solves the issue – wrong taps in the wrong combination!?! The water is cool but very refreshing.

With not knowing where we are we take the hotel tuk-tuk downtown to Pub Street and our first taste of Siem Reap by night; very vibrant and lively. We wander around the narrow streets looking for somewhere to eat, finally being tempted into a restaurant called Karo by a young friendly local. Only right that we try the local food so we order the lok lak beef and a chicken with cashew nuts dish, both delicious and with a free beer each thrown in as well, a perfect start to the evening.

We explore the small Pub Street area further before settling in a bar down one of the side streets, what with decent music, comfortable seats and beer at fifty cents (half a dollar) plus popcorn …. we are in heaven! Alison decides to push the boat out and orders gin and tonic for one whole dollar! By the end of the night, we have a bar tab for five drinks of three dollars, (about £2 in English). We negotiate a tuk-tuk ride home, again the driver does not seem sure where it is but we get there, again following a conversation with another local.

10th November

We are both awake early, not the best night's sleep. No air-conditioning but instead a noisy fan. We head down for breakfast where we are presented with a list of options, one meal and one drink. For ease we both opt for the scrambled egg and bread, which turns out to be a foot long baguette. The coffee accompanying the breakfast is just the job, very strong and tasty. With breakfast completed we hand over our dirty washing at reception, they weigh it and we are charged by the kilo, each kilo costs one dollar.

Having got our bearings of where the town is from last night's journey in the dark, we decide to walk and explore for ourselves. We find our way no problem so can check out the bus and tour options, for both local attractions and for our onward travel. We discover the old market, lots of stalls selling lots of smelly dried fish and other things unknown to us. There is a river running through the town so we follow that for a while and decide that we will come back another day as there are a few temples about that we are not suitably dressed for this morning. The big hand on the clock strikes beer and we find a bar that serves it in frosted glasses straight from the freezer, again just fifty cents; so refreshing on a day like this.

We walk back to our hotel, and as we turn the corner we see our washing drying out on the roof! The pool entices us, so its upstairs to get changed into swimming attire. By the time we go back to our room our washing has been returned, all neatly folded. Alison notices that the top sheet of our bed is actually a duvet cover, minus the duvet – so you could sleep in it sleeping bag style if you liked. Shower successfully mastered and a third walk of the day as we head once again into town for our tea.

With a couple of beers on the way we again visit Karo's for another satisfying meal and accompanying free beer. Being creatures of habit, we sit in the same relaxing bar we visited last night. We chat with an American couple whose travel plans make ours seem tame; they are not planning to return home for two years! Next stop for them is house-sitting for someone in the Seychelles for two months. Whilst we are sitting enjoying our beers, we are amused by the locals who are eating snakes on a stick, we had noticed that the local street vendors serve up a good array of spiders and crickets also; yum…

When we settle our bar bill, we discover that although everything is priced up in American dollars change is given out in Cambodian riels, or sometimes a combination of the two. So, hand over five dollars for a two-dollar fifty cent bill you need to be aware of all the permutations that your change could be returned in.

11th November

After a better night's sleep we are about in good time as it is a busy day ahead. Today, we expect, will be one of the highlights of our whole time away, Angkor Wat. Today's breakfast of choice is a fried egg baguette washed down with a banana milkshake; excellent.

At eight o' clock we depart with the hotel tuk-tuk driver, Sok, and head to Angkor, it is just a short journey of about four or so miles. We opt for the three days pass as have been advised that it is impossible to squeeze all the sights into a single day. Without going into all the history and details it is fair to say that our expectations were exceeded, we are completely blown away with what had been built over eight hundred years ago, and is the largest temple complex in the world.

If Angkor Wat is the iconic image with its magnificent bayons then Angkor Thom is equally stunning, giant faces looking in all directions, it is hard to imagine the craftsmanship that has gone into these and how it was all put in place with no mechanical aides. We followed that with Ta Prohm, most famous to many people for the Tomb Raider films, massive temples that have become overgrown over hundreds of years, where tree roots have attached themselves in impossible places; bizarre. Adding to the experience is the fact that they are working temples and hundreds of monks in their bright orange robes are wandering around.

The carvings are incredible, and we cannot comprehend what it would have been like in its day when hundreds of thousands of people would have been going about their daily routines. So much had been destroyed in the Pol Pot regime, mainly Gods having their heads knocked off, but other carvings look like they could have been done yesterday. When you think that you can no longer be impressed further you turn another corner to be left open-mouthed again.

The sights and camera opportunities are endless, unfortunately so are the selfie-sticks. There will be no need for a gym visit after a day here, we would not like to guess at the number of steps that we have climbed up (and back down). Health and safety rules just do not exist here, there are no safety rails, and most people like us are doing it in sandals and flip-flops. We are full of admiration of the stamina of the older visitors, we are giving a lot of people twenty plus years and with the heat we are completely shattered ourselves.

Sok has been an excellent guide, though he does have the habit of always being asleep whenever we get back to the tuk-tuk! As soon as we get out and start viewing temples, he takes the opportunity to get his hammock strung out in the back for forty winks. To finish the day, he takes us to a viewing point for the sunset, along with thousands of others. It is a long climb but worth it in the end and is a fitting ending to our first day at Angkor Wat. Having watched the sun go down all that is left before returning to the hotel is the long walk back down the hill in near darkness!

Back to base and a quick shower then out for the evening. We opt for the same bar as last night, Mikey's, for pre-dinner beers. We have our suspicions that there might be more than liquid refreshment on offer here as there are several scantily clad local ladies arriving. Oh well, each to their own! We need cash before dinner so following a Tripadvisor tip we head to the Maybank ATM to try our luck – yes, the Norwich & Peterborough debit card is accepted with no charge. When you are on a budget you want to save money where you can and ATM charges soon add up. It pays to do your research. Karos once more for dinner as it has been so good, however service was poor tonight. We call it a night, and negotiate a tuk-tuk home for a dollar.

12th November

I had the best breakfast this morning, a cheese omelette in a baguette, Alison was quite envious as her cheese & green tomatoes did not really come up to scratch. The banana shakes are awesome though.

More temples are on the agenda this morning, Sok picks us up at eight thirty. We venture further into the Angkor complex to visit Ta Keo, Preah Khan, Neak Pean (surrounded by water), Ta Som, East Mebon and finally Pre Rup. We have seen enough of the temples now, but as we had spent longer periods between each one travelling, we get to see more of the countryside which was great. Multiple stops also gave Sok a chance to catch up on some sleep as on our return to the tuk-tuk each time we have to wake him up!

An amusing observation is that stall holders at each temple are selling the same water for the same price, they all rush towards you, how do you choose? I usually go for the cutest smile; it does make you feel wanted though.

We decide on a relaxing trip to the Tonle Sap Lake this afternoon. After a long, bumpy and dusty tuk-tuk ride and paying out twenty dollars each, we realise that we have made the first mistake of our trip so far. We were on the boat for little over an hour and it soon became clear this was a total tourist trap. Transported to a floating village including a fish and crocodile farm, our 'guide' then suggested that we buy rice for the local school children, not just your average size bag, we are talking a hessian sack priced at fifty dollars! So, all in all its a bit of a con, but it was another guide book tick!

Back at the hotel and after a bit more fiddling with the shower, hot water is eventually discovered!

As it has been raining whilst we were getting ready to go out, we make use of Sok's tuk-tuk services again for a trip into town. With nothing much planned for tomorrow we decide to try the street food tonight, very tasty noodles they are too. Drinks at the Cocktail Bar, where they promptly run out of beer. Cocktails it is then, Black Russian & Gin Fizz are an adequate substitute. We share a table with an English guy and his extremely attractive Cambodian partner, decide he is batting well above his average!

13th November

It's a leisurely wake-up this morning as no specific plans made for today, we soon realise that it is pouring with rain so just as well. Pity the group we heard getting up at 5 a.m. for a sunrise excursion.

A leisurely breakfast of omelettes and coffee followed with a relax (undercover) by the pool. More games of scrabble. With the rain having subsided we decide to walk into town and have a wander. We check out bus prices and menus, which is thirsty work so have to stop off for beers. Killing time around the indoor market we peruse a few stalls and come across a nice painting, although we are just unsure how well it will travel home rolled up for so long, one to ponder. Whilst we have an iced coffee a young girl sells us post cards that we do not really need, so we decide to go 'old school' and send one home to Mum and Dad. We buy a stamp for a dollar and put the card in a wooden box, we will see what happens.

The Doctor Fish pedicure looks enticing, perhaps even try one before we leave? Black clouds are again beginning to loom above so we head back to base, relax by the pool and play more Scrabble! The rain does not come...

We walk into town tonight via the Night Market route. We discover the Bugs Café, but not sure we are that brave. It does have to be said that the menu is interesting to say the least! There are diverse options, from light snacks of 'insect tapas' for those not that hungry - think silkworms, ants and grasshoppers. If you have a bigger appetite, how about a trio of scorpions on a bed of papaya salad? For those not keen on salad how about the tarantula donut? Personally, I see that more as a desert. The restaurant we decide on is great, and whilst plenty of lizards may be on the ceiling and walls, they are not garnishing the dish! Both the fish amok and chicken amok we opt for are superb. Over our meal we chat to a couple who have just been to Laos, it sounded interesting but more research required for that one. They had also been to Phnom Penh and give us some tips about excursions and safety, making it sound a bit grim, but we will reserve judgement rather than arrive with pre-conceived expectations. As with all of this trip we travel with an open mind.

14th November

Upon waking up this morning and flicking on the antiquated TV the news is all about a terrorist attack in France. Across Paris one hundred plus people have lost their lives, many in a concert hall but others just murdered in various restaurants around the city. A very sombre and depressing start to the day.

A couple of black coffees wash down our now 'regular' breakfast of omelette in a baguette, maybe it's the freshness of ingredients but such a simple option is delicious.

With blue skies all around we walk into Siem Reap to pick off various recommendations from the guide book. The world-famous Raffles Hotel chain now presides over the Grand Hotel d'Angkor, dating back to the 1930s it has a guest list of the rich and famous – Charlie Chaplin, Princess Margaret, Roger Moore and Bill Clinton to name just a few. Away from the celebrity list it has a prominent part in Cambodian history as the location for the signing of the 1991 Paris Peace Agreement, bringing a brighter future to the whole country. Considering it is part of the Raffles chain it was looking a little tired, with overgrown gardens and broken fountains - it hardly screamed luxury.

Walking alongside the river back into the centre of Siem we see two groups of rowers in longboats, some local guy who speaks half-decent English tells us that they are in training for the annual longboat races that are due soon.

The temples are abundant with colour, our list takes in Wat Kerararam, Preah Ang Chek and Preah Ang Chom. Wat Kerararam has fabulous stories, both on the walls in picture form but also using statues and depictions in the grounds. It is also known by the serene sounding name Pagoda of the Cornflower Petals. It is stunningly beautiful but behind all the colour and flowers is the grim reality that it once housed a security office, prison and a killing field in the days of the Pol Pot regime. As recently as 2012 a mass grave had been discovered at this very site. Wat Preah Prohm Rath was also very good and has its own unique story involving a monk, his daily collecting of rice, crocodiles and vultures. It is all told in full technicolour, entrails displayed, the works! A couple more temples will have to wait for another day – closed!

It seems the opportune time for liquid refreshments and some light shopping, beers and T-shirts! What started out as a sunny morning ends with us getting caught in the rain as we return to the hostel, fortunately the rain is on the warm side and quite refreshing.

With the weather having cleared up we walk back into town, before eating we again look at the painting that we really like in one of the many night markets. Over another simple but delicious meal we mull it over and decide to risk taking it home, with sixteen dollars agreed the lady rolls up our painting and puts it into a rattan-type tube, fingers crossed it survives the remainder of the journey.

With the cocktail bar from the other evening being closed we end up sat in what has become our 'regular' haunt. We get chatting to a couple from Essex who now live in Thailand six months of the year, over the course of the conversation we discover that they are originally from Sibsey, a little village six miles from our own home town – it really is a small world! An early night for us as another trip to the Angkor complex in the morning.

15th November

Why do we never sleep as well when the alarm is set? We are up in good time and with breakfasts devoured we are back on the road. No Sok today as he is busy – no sun either, stormy skies overhead.

It is a long ride out today; we are heading to the Rolous group of Temples and our first stop is over an hour away. Right on cue the heavens open just as we park up at Banteay Srei, the ever-opportunistic locals are quickly over with ponchos for sale!

Banteay Srei is one of the most elaborate temples and dedicated to the Hindu god Shiva, dating back to the tenth century. It is famous for its beautiful pinkish sandstone and intricate three-dimensional wall carvings. The name means 'Citadel of Women' and many believe that the delicate carvings may well have been done entirely by female sculptors. The sandstone of which it is constructed is softer than many materials and can be carved like wood. It is a shame for us that we are looking at it in the pouring rain, rather than viewing it in scorching sunlight where the pick hues would add to its beauty.

The Temples we take in today - Banteay Samre, Lolei, and Preah Ko are all amazing, but having viewed their more famous counterparts on our first excursion into the Angkor complex we are becoming blasé about today's sights. What is intriguing is the ride through the countryside and seeing the locals go about their daily business. The hairdressers, completely open sided but with the chair just like at home, pigs wallowing in ponds, ducks and chickens being kept for their eggs, and no doubt meat. The children all seem so happy waving at us as we speed through village after village.

By 1 p.m. we are back at the hostel, our banana milkshakes barely touch the side as we rehydrate following this morning's excursion.

We have a quick dip before heading to reception to book our onward travel to Battambang. With that in hand we can relax, so head into town for a meal. The burger bar we first stop at is expensive for food so we just have a beer each and move on to where we ate last night. The beef lok lak is equally as good as the time before.

As dusk falls, we promenade down the riverside, admiring the lit-up bridges and waterwheel, when you see the town as picturesque as this it is hard to imagine the horrors that it has gone through within our own lifetimes. We settle down for cocktails, well why not when they are only a dollar each! Mojitos and Beach Monkeys, followed by a few gins and beers. What started as us going out early evening in daylight ends with us having to wake Sok up from his hammock to let us in through the locked gates! Sods law that on our latest night out we get woken by noisy guests in the early hours of the morning.

16th November

Headaches all around this morning, but luckily nothing omelettes and black coffee cannot sort out. We are obviously not with-it today; we have locked ourselves out of the room – in all honesty cannot believe that it is only the first time.

It is our last day in Siem Reap, nothing much doing so we head out to the pool for what we plan as a lazy day. Two hours (and two banana milkshakes) later we are both as fit as fiddles so we head off in search of Wat Bo, one of the Temples that was closed on our last visit. Surprise-surprise, its closed again, obviously the Wat of 'the Lazy Monk'. It is not a completely wasted journey as we pop to the bank and have another delicious iced coffee – they taste so good that they can't be good for the waistline?

To get our bigger notes change we head to the supermarket, (toothpaste, Panadol required), where we are super impressed with the checkouts. As each item is scanned in addition to the description, it also shows a picture – and we think we are ahead of some of these countries... With our fifty-dollar note broken down into smaller denominations we head to our favourite daytime bar where the heavy pint glasses come directly out of the freezer. With the mercury constantly sitting around the thirty degrees mark it is just the job.

We get chatting to a lady from Cumbria, England – she is using her leave from our National Health Service to work for a nursing charity at a hospital in Battambang where we are heading next. Her insight into Cambodian health care is harrowing. Single-use equipment reused repeatedly, but generally there is a complete lack of training and limited know how, hospital treatment over here is best avoided! She does advise us that the Handa hospital in Battambang is the place to go, some Dutch doctor oversees the day to day running and it is supposedly the best in Cambodia. She gives us a few more tips and as we leave we settle her bar bill along with ours, it is our good deed for the day, nothing in comparison to the time and knowledge that she is passing on in trying to improve their medical care.

Finally, we get the fish massage that we had promised ourselves the other day, it was very tickly to start with but enjoyable by the finish. We leave with the cleanest, softest feet we have had for a long while!

With it being our final night in Siem Reap we eat at our favourite place, unfortunately the rice we are served is cold but they soon correct that. To wash down our meal we head to the Angkor Famous Cocktail bar where the bartender remembered our order from the previous night – must be time for us to move on. Next door there is the most horrific Karaoke singing going on that we have ever heard, it is not musically entertaining but high in the comedy stakes.

Tomorrow we are back on the move.

Battambang

17th November

Another good night's sleep and we are awake in plenty of time for a relaxing, final breakfast at the Yellow Hostel. The kitchen stock control seems to have failed this morning though, there is an egg shortage! With plenty of chickens around the crisis is swiftly averted, a good strong coffee but in moderation today, a long bus journey ahead.

We bring our bags downstairs and checkout, waiting in reception for nine thirty as per bus pick-up instructions. We need not have rushed as a good forty-five minutes pass before the initial battered mini-bus transfers us to the bus station. The main bus is a slight improvement, the seat back is very dodgy but not as bad as some of the stories we have heard. The 'No Durian' sign is prominently displayed; this fruit obviously has one bad reputation - its smell is that offensive! Travelling today is a good mix of tourists and locals, with a lot of young babies in the local category. After a further round of pick-ups, we finally get on our way by eleven thirty. Not sure who designed the décor for this bus, lots of gaudy, frilly curtains and Buddha images. The TV at the front is showing some Vin Diesel film and the volume is very loud...

After about an hour of travel the bus pulls over for a ten-minute refreshment stop. When the locals return the snack of the day appears to be bags of fried crickets. The lady opposite us has pushed the boat out, corn on the cob, sticky bamboo rice and a bag of crickets! The driver is a bit horn happy, and if it is not the sound of his horn it is his mobile phone ringing – this guy is in big demand... There seems to be random pick-ups and drop-offs for locals on route and at one point the driver stops to do his shopping! Overall, not a bad journey, one to use as a benchmark and if nothing worse than this one we are more than happy.

We arrive in Battambang just before three, so not that far away from the time we expected. There is a tuk-tuk frenzy at the bus station, the local drivers obviously know exactly what time the buses arrive and they waste no time in targeting the tourists. Whether it is by luck or good business practise the guy who approaches us, Yaya, offers free transfers to our hotel. On the short journey we are shown all the trips that he offers, their prices and we are given his business card. On arrival at the Hotel Asia we are pleasantly surprised, and discover that Yaya really is affiliated to the hotel.

Exploring the town while daylight remains is the next mission, we find the market, albeit nearly sold out of stock but that is no surprise at this time of day. We manage to pick up a leaflet with a map for walking tours, so tomorrows plan is to get our bearings and then we will book excursions with Yaya for either Thursday or Friday, possibly both? Back to the hotel for a freshen up, cold water only; despite it initially taking your breath away it is an enjoyable shower and we feel recharged. Standard Asian toiletries included, the world's smallest bar of soap and a pair of white flimsy plastic toothbrushes.

As it turns to dusk we head out for food by the riverside. There are lots of little stalls, it is table service with menus and the food is cooked fresh in front of you, so what is not to like? The food is good but not overly exciting, Cambodian food undeniably lacks the taste sensation that we experienced in Thailand, but it is cheap and filling – we really should not complain. Across the river is the Sky Bar that the nurse we met in Siem Reap recommended, considering it is quite a luxurious setting the bar prices are very reasonable. It offers a splendid view over the town on the other side. We opt for an early night; evening entertainment is extremely low key here compared to Siem Reap – a few quiet nights will do us good.

18th November

With no breakfast included at our hotel first task of the morning is to find some food. The river stalls are not open in the morning, so that option does not exist. Down the side of the market, on the opposite side of the road is a place called 'Sweet Coffee', so we try there. We both order coffee and are promptly served a jasmine tea! It turns out that this is free and it is for you to drink whilst the coffee brews and filters at your table. The flaw of this is that the coffee takes so long to pass through the filters it is just luke-warm – we will be searching for a different, and hopefully better breakfast option for tomorrow.

Back across the road and the market is in full flow, and it is not for the squeamish. Cambodian ladies squat down while butchering anything that moves, well maybe that is a slight exaggeration! Fish are decapitated at a speedy rate, frogs separated from their legs on the next stall. We can vouch for the freshness as they are still alive whilst they are being dismembered, the fish are still moving even whilst they are being filleted. One of the less gruesome jobs is to 'waft', this can be a hankie or feather duster but the aim is the same – disperse the flies!

Away from the butchery department is a stall selling various cakes, we have no idea what they are as no English spoken at all by the stallholder. We opt for three different cakes and the lady shows us how much we owe her by holding up a note (of the money variety). On the taste test, two of the three are disappointing whilst the third was ok and we would have again.

Having been fed we head back on our self-guided walking tour which takes in several of the town's bridges, and more interestingly the French architecture from a bygone era. Some of the buildings are extremely attractive in design and very well maintained... other parts of the town are quite run down. Opportunity arises for an ice cream so we take full advantage, we have not seen many places selling them. Overall, it takes us a good couple of hours to wander around

Cambodia's second city; that gives you an idea that it is just not that big! There seems to be a lot of schools here, perhaps those who have a little bit more wealth are educated here rather than in their local villages?

Always planning ahead, we keep one eye out for the Capitol Bus station / booking office, that is something we need to get booked for our onward travel come Saturday. Failing in that mission we come across a bar / restaurant called the White Rose, its one that is mentioned in all the guidebooks so we treat ourselves to a snack of sweet potato chips and a couple of well-earned beers. Whilst in here we get chatting to another couple, this time there from Lincoln – so not quite on our doorstep but still very local to our home town.

Once back at the hotel we book Yaya for one of his excursions tomorrow. A full day trip split into two halves, avoiding the midday heat. We are very much looking forward to being ferried around – it will give our aching legs a rest while we are sat relaxing in the tuk-tuk, a warm breeze in our faces. Whilst chatting to Yaya he explains to us what a young country Cambodia is age wise, seventy five percent of its population have been born since 1979 – equally astonishing as it is frightening. It really brings home how many of its population were murdered by the Khmer Rouge.

Following at least a dozen nights of either rice or noodles we find a pizza option! Not the standard fare of ham and pineapple but the slightly more exotic option of crab and chicken. They were a taste sensation, the crab one especially flavoursome. Our visit to the Sky Bar is curtailed, not sure what has happened tonight, but its bug central. Something to do with the weather? Either way we are not happy, so drink up and leave - such a shame as they give you a small bowl of nuts with every drink order. By 10 p.m. the shutters are coming down across the city so we call it a day.

19th November

The pizza from last night has left us full, it can only be the change to the diet so we manage without breakfast. One discovery from yesterday's walk was a lovely little coffee shop just across the road from our hotel. It has just the four tables set up outside and the building is very ornate, so we order coffee... and then get tempted with the home-made scones that are on the menu! Huge thumbs up from us both and it is safe to say we have found our new breakfast location of choice.

Crossing the road back to the hotel and Yaya is already there, bang on time. We collect a couple of bottles of water from reception and we are off. First stop is the old railway station; a quite simple but attractive building with a large clock on the outside. Yaya tells us how the Khmer Rouge closed the station as they did not want anyone leaving the city. Not happy at just closing the station they then proceed with setting landmines along the tracks just in case people decide to leave on foot. The clock is showing a couple of minutes past eight, the very time that the last train left.

Having left one railway station we head out of the city to where the famous 'Bamboo' train runs. These days it is very much a tourist attraction, but at one point it ran all the way to the capital Phnom Penh. In total now, it is about five miles long, and heads to the next village whose whole economy probably comes from T-shirts and souvenir sales. The bamboo train or 'Nori' to use its local name is an amazingly simple device, a pair of axles, a framework with a flatbed made from bamboo and a small motorcycle or tractor engine. The line is single track, but trains run in both directions simultaneously, the rule of thumb being that the train carrying least passengers must stop and be lifted off the track! Assembly, and removal, of these trains can be done in a minute. The driver tells us that the lines were going to be upgraded and a proper service be put in place between Battambang and Phnom Penh, whilst that is obviously progress it is such a shame that such a unique experience will disappear for good.

With that explanation straw mats were put on the bamboo and we get aboard sitting cross-legged. In no time we were speeding through the countryside, the tracks did not look very safe, not always parallel to each other and sometimes small gaps between where one rail (nearly) joined the other. Just to add to the drama there was some huge black and yellow spiders that had inconsiderately knitted their webs at head height, a few cows and oncoming traffic. What a fantastic experience, so once we got to the village at the far end, I was more than happy to buy the T-shirt! The journey back was less eventful, no train heading in the opposite direction, the cows had moved elsewhere and we were better prepared for the cobwebs and huge spiders.

Yaya is waiting for us on our return and gives us a bit more of an insight into the history, of how the train used to run from village to village and was originally propelled by the driver using a bamboo pole, I guess like how a punt works. The engines that are currently being used were donated by the United Nations at the end of the Pol Pot era. No doubt the poor man who used to power it with a bamboo pole was over the moon! One small footnote, the couple from Lincoln were here again! It is such a small city and the attractions that people are here for tend to be the same ones; lots of people are beginning to look familiar. With this morning's excursion concluded Yaya runs us back to Battambang, kindly dropping us at the Capitol bus office, it is just a hundred metres from our hotel, but behind the main street which we have walked down numerous times.

After a freshen up and water intake we head out in search of something to eat. As much as the heat suppresses your appetite, we have only eaten a scone each today so far! We head to yesterday's cake lady and her small stall, today opting for a pair of new cakes. One of the two is very tasty and flaky with an iced tattoo style design on top – no idea what that is meant to represent. The other is unremarkable.

Continuing our walk down the riverside we come across a group of boys (young men) fishing. They have a weighted net which they throw out like a large lasso, it goes with the tide for twenty metres or so where they retrieve it, and hopefully a fish or two. They were getting some success in the time we spent watching, maybe that's tonights tea sorted? We stop at the Ambrosia; another little restaurant come bar and have a beer before heading back to the hotel ready for part two of today's excursion.

Yaya is late picking us up, he has had a puncture. The worst part of the wait is trying to fend off all the other tuk-tuk drivers who are trying to poach his customers. Before too long he appears so we are on the road heading out of Battambang to the chillingly named Killing Cave at Phnom Sampeau. This is one of just many of the Khmer Rouge execution sites in this region, locals estimate that around ten thousand people met their deaths here. There was no discretion or sympathy shown; men, women and children all met the same fate.

From the bottom of the hill where we are parked it is a long hike up to the top, but our efforts are saved by the couple from Lincoln who we have been chatting too on our multiple meetings; they have hired a jeep and driver, so for the cost of a beer later tonight we have a lift up the hill sorted! Half way up the road we reach the temple and cave, leading up to the cave are statues depicting the horrendous torture methods of the Khmer soldiers. Entering inside and it is all very eerie as it houses a large wire cage full of bones and skulls. At the top of the limestone cave is a natural skylight, which is where the Khmer Rouge soldiers marched people to, lining them up, bludgeoning them and letting their bodies fall into the darkness below. It is terrifying to think that those in the queue knew their fate and had no option other than wait for the inevitable. Of course, not everyone who had been struck over the head had been killed outright; the fall was certain to finish off the majority. If you survived the initial blow and your fall was cushioned by the dozens of bodies who had gone before you, starvation would eventually put you out of your misery.

Stepping out of the shade and back into the sunshine it is hard to square in your head; the beauty of the views across the countryside, macaque monkeys playing around the stunning Temple but knowing just a few metres away such cruelty and murder have taken place. We spend thirty minutes or so just looking across the green plains back towards Battambang, exploring the temple and enjoying watching the monkeys climb the drainpipes and swing from the roofs.

The bat caves are next for us, we find a suitable viewing spot and there are plenty of vendors selling drinks, snacks, souvenirs etc. to the daily hordes. I take the opportunity to taste my first ever cricket, not unpleasant by any means – prawny, nutty, deep fried sort of vibe. Wouldn't convert me away from a bag of cheese and onion crisps though...

Right on cue, and apparently you can almost set your clock by them the bats start flooding out of the caves, it really is quite a spectacle. We leave after about twenty minutes and there is no sign of the display finishing any time soon, we are led to believe that it takes about forty minutes in total for all the bats to exit, strangely no-one seems to know when they all return!

With darkness all around we head for home, Yaya spots a huge snake in the road, no sooner has he pointed it out to us and it has gone into the long grass at the side of the road. Yaya is not having his finest day with his vehicle, having sorted the puncture out earlier it now has a refusal to start after a trip to the petrol station – we have a temporary vision of walking the remainder of the route home; luckily with some assistance the engine is back running. Yaya is in a good mood; he has more work booked in for tomorrow.

Showered and changed, fed for under two dollars each we make our way to Ambrosia to meet the couple from Lincoln. We have a good night chatting about travel experiences until we are turned out; quarter past ten seems to be about last orders in these parts. We walk home without seeing another soul about!

20th November

With all these early nights it is no surprise that they are followed by early mornings! With a coffee down us we head to the cake lady for our breakfast, not the most nutritious, but hey we are on our holidays. Through the process of narrowing down which cakes we are not enamoured with we end up with three excellent ones today – we take these to the river and sit on a bench watching the world go by.

To give our legs a proper stretch we head to the roundabout which is home to the iconic symbol of Battambang, or at least unforgettable to anyone who has ever visited here. Lok Ta Dumbong is the guy who is depicted, complete with his stick, and even today he is seen as the saviour of the city. Offerings of fruit and flowers are made daily – which means people park up on the roundabout, get out of their vehicles to pray and leave gifts, maybe his super powers extend to preventing road traffic collisions? The legend says that he thwarted the King with his magic stick and saved the town; we will leave the story at that point as there are so many more myths, (flying white horses, monks and disappearing acts, perhaps an early Cambodian magician?).

For the first time during our time here the Museum is open, so with a princely sum of a one-dollar entry fee we head across the bridge to have a morning of education. The first part of the museum houses various relics, broken crockery and parts of carvings – nothing we haven't seen before. The second part is a fascinating exhibition, detailing stories of local families during their forced relocation under Khmer rule. Pol Pot, and his ideals are far too complicated (and grim) to go into in a travel diary, but for anyone interested in travelling to Cambodia it is well worth reading up about – and it is frightening that the rest of the world turned a blind-eye to what was happening here during the 1970s. The museum brought home the local impact, lots of accounts were from individuals living in the local streets that we have walked down; some had happy conclusions where they were eventually reunited, but sadly the majority were stories of immense loss.

Upon leaving the museum we fail again to find the Boxing Stadium, using the word stadium suggests it ought to be of a size that cannot be missed, but it is beyond us to locate it. Maybe it is just a little gym that has given itself a grand name? While in this part of town we revisit the train station, the sun is in a better place for photographs than when we visited with Yaya for the first time. An ice-cold beer before we head back to base, bags to pack ready for moving on in the morning.

Come early evening we go in search of food for the long bus journey to Phnom Penh, our biggest issue is that there does not seem to be such a thing as a supermarket anywhere around here! Baguettes are sourced from a local bakery and from the petrol station we purchase that international food saviour, a tube of Pringles.

Our last evening in Battambang is a strange experience, over the last few nights we thought the quantity of bugs was increasing – tonight there has been a critter explosion! The food market stalls have turned out their lights, cooking and eating in near darkness is preferable to being battered by insects that a switched-on light attracts. The fried rice seemed extra delicious tonight, maybe it contained unseen added ingredients?

Phnom Penh

21st November

Check-out time today is before our usual rise, fortunately our favourite coffee shop across the road is open so we are able to bring ourselves around gently.

Amazingly we are picked up on time and taken out to the bigger bus station (and bigger bus) on the outskirts of the city. Surprisingly we are the only white faces making this journey, it seems from chatting to people most have been on a route from Phnom Penh heading north, where we are doing it the other way around as Vietnam is next on our agenda. The bus journey is bottom-numbingly long, the road condition being the biggest factor in that, incredibly bumpy. With three stops along the way we supplement our very dry baguettes with pineapple. Other highlights of the journey (if that is the correct word); a flatbed lorry heavily laden with dead chickens - from a distance it had looked like just a load of feathers, a Cambodian version of X-Factor (mainly singing) and an old Sylvester Stallone film. Entertainment every step of the way...

The final trail into Phnom Penh is the worst, but maybe good news for anyone making the journey in a year or twos time. Roadworks everywhere mean that the last ninety minutes of the journey are akin to driving through a building site. After seven hours we eventually arrive in Phnom Penh and manage to negotiate with a tuk-tuk driver for our onward travel to the luxuriously named Blue Home Villa. The driver does not know exactly where it is, but is familiar with the streets in the vicinity of the Royal Palace so soon manages to locate it. It does not meet with our interpretation of the word 'Villa', but then again it was hardly likely to on our budget!

The Blue Home Villa is run by a young couple, early twenties at a guess? They also speak the best English of anyone we have met so far, which is handy in regards to getting our laundry sorted and onward travel. The room is the smallest we have ever stayed in, just the width of a bed meaning the only way into it is from the foot end, a tiny bathroom and stiflingly hot!

With it already turning dark we do not venture too far from home tonight. Our location means we cannot get lost – we are one street away from the Palace and just across the road is the river. On the street facing the river is restaurant after restaurant, all serving the same limited menu. The food was ok, but the beer was cheap and cold so not all bad. By the time we return our accommodation is all in darkness, luckily the young lady is still about though, so we manage to get some bottles of water. A definite plus to this stay, in our small room and on our small TV there is a football channel! On the downside it is yet another stop with no hot water.

22nd November

Even though our room is in pitch darkness (there are no windows at all, just rooms off a long corridor), we are awake early. The only light to be seen at all is the red dot of the TV standby.

Once up and about our first thought is how few people there are around here! The streets are noticeably quiet considering we are in the capital city. Today we are looking to visit the Tuol Sleng S21 Genocide Museum, but before getting there we really need coffee and breakfast, or at least food of some kind. Before too long we find a coffee shop, but no food. Just when it looks like buying a pack of biscuits is the most likely outcome, we find an old lady selling fresh donuts! The smell is incredible and the donuts do not disappoint, in fact we would probably go as far as declaring them the finest donuts we have ever tasted! Could the secret be that they have been fried in coconut oil...

As we approach the gates to Tuol Sleng there are a lot more people about, visitors arriving by minibuses and tuk-tuks. Over the next three hours we look around and read about the grim reality that met anyone who was unfortunate enough to be held here. What was formerly a school was converted into a detention centre, the classrooms into cells and torture chambers. The whole place was surrounded by electrified barbed wire and nets hanging from upstairs floors meant that committing suicide to end your misery was impossible.

Estimates suggest that around twenty thousand people passed through here between 1976 and 1979, and this is just one (albeit the most famous) of about two hundred similar facilities used under the regime. Life here was spent mainly chained up, that was as good as it got; if you were removed from your shackles that would most likely to be tortured, to get forced confessions from you, agreeing to whatever charges they have you held in there for. Food was minimal; four small spoonsful of rice and watery leaves each day was the best you could hope for. In the early months bodies were buried near the prison, but within the year there was no space left. From that point on the Khmer Rouge would walk the detainees the ten miles to what have since become known as the Killing Fields.

In some of the classroom's come cells are row after row of photographs of people who fell victim to the regime. Age was no barrier, their theory was that if you are to cut a lawn it needs constant attention, whereas if you take it out from the roots that is the job done for good. For the word 'lawn' they meant families, rather than leaving angry parents, partners or children behind, they just murdered the whole lot. There is the odd harrowing account of survival amongst the photos, but these were from people who were of use to the detention centre, they had skills, maybe in repairing machinery. Of the twenty thousand estimated to have passed through the prison there are only twelve known survivors, plus a further twenty-three who were being detained there when it was liberated in January 1979.

Strangely from the moment we step out of the gates it is as if a switch has been flicked; life is going on as normal, locals smiling and laughing, trying to sell you trips to the Killing Fields as if you have not experienced enough death and destruction for one day. We will visit, but not today.

We wander back towards the city and the river, and go to visit a colourful temple, Wat Phnom. It is an attractive Buddhist temple, situated on a small hill and offers magnificent views across the streets nearby. Its name means Mountain Pagoda, so very fitting. It has a large clock set into the gardens on one side of the grounds and it is a calm place in the now bustling city. Heading back towards the Palace we explore some of the streets by the river in preparation for our meal tonight, now we are familiar with our whereabouts there are plenty of options.

Back at the Blue Home Villa we arrange a bus to take us to Kampot in a few days' time, our laundry has not yet been returned – fortunately, we still have odd items left to wear! We shower, quickly as the water is cold, and get changed to go back out – it is a long while since those donuts this morning. We eat on the river front at a place called the Pink Elephant, the food is tasty (still rice and noodles though). Further along we had seen a 'Skybar' advertising an open-air roof top seating area. Our weary legs groan as we head up the three flights of stairs, but the effort is worth it. There are good views across the river, a lovely breeze, and no bugs at all!

23rd November

We wake up a little later than some days, the dark windowless room has played its part no doubt. As we set off to leave in search of a breakfast we are greeted by the smiley proprietor with our clean laundry, it is all nicely packed and folded – sometimes it has been returned more crumpled than when we sent it away...

Last night we had spotted somewhere doing a buffet breakfast, but this morning we cannot find it! With a full feast out of the question we opt for baguettes and coffee – not what we had been hoping for but it has left us satisfied and cost next to nothing. We chat to the guy who serves us breakfast and he advises us that a tuk-tuk to the Killing Field should cost no more than twelve or thirteen dollars, its handy to know that as the drivers always start as high as they can, hoping you have no idea of what is the going rate.

With our new found information we negotiate a ride out to the Killing Field of Cheung Ek. It is a forty-five-minute ride out of the city, the roads are very dusty, but it is so nice to be out of the heat and feel the breeze in your face. On arrival it is hard to believe what you are about to witness; you are in what appears to be a nice part of the countryside – indeed many years ago it was the site of an orchard. Outside the entrance there are people selling coconuts, a school next door, the only clue to the recent history of this place is the sign at the entrance, "Chokung Ek Genocidal Centre".

This is the most 'infamous' of all the Killing Fields in Cambodia. In the years since 1979 around 1.4 million bodies buried across twenty thousand different Killing Field sites have been found across the country. Cheung Ek is by far the largest of them all; just under nine thousand people were executed and then buried here at Cheung Ek. It is thought most, if not all of these will have been brought across from Tuol Sleng (S21) where we had visited yesterday, so many faces from those photographs we saw yesterday will have met their death in this very field.

Cheung Ek is a memorial site, marked by a Buddhist Stupa with glass sides. Unremarkable until you get closer and see that the Stupa is filled with more than five thousand human skulls. Some of the lower levels are opened during the day so that the skulls can be seen directly. Many of the skulls have been shattered or smashed in, they were killed by a group of teenagers led by a Senior Khmer Comrade. Ammunition was scarce and expensive, so prisoners were made to kneel before being battered with iron bars, pickaxes, machetes and any other makeshift weapon. The bodies were then piled into mass graves.

The audio tour is particularly good, it guides you around the site and explains what is in front of you, mass graves where fragments of bones and items of clothing still breach the surface to this day. Whilst the entire place is harrowing, the 'killing tree' is the most chilling. This tree was used to smash the skulls of babies and young children until they met with their inevitable death. A tannoy system within the museum plays music and Khmer propaganda broadcasts, this would have been used to hide the noise of the dying.

Both here and Tuol Sleng are places that you must visit when in Cambodia, as much as you can learn from history or guidebooks there is nothing like seeing the places for yourself, only then can you imagine the true horror of what went on so recently in such a beautiful country.

24th November

After seeing the darker side of Phnom Penh, it is a lighter day planned for today; nothing more on our itinerary than the Central Market and a good wander around - obviously starting with breakfast. We find a bar with a hostel attached, as well as offering breakfasts it also has a more 'Western' style menu including burgers and chips, so maybe that could be tonights meal sorted out too. Peanut butter and toast, plus coffee; just the job to start the day and we have not had peanut butter for ages!

The Central Market is a stunning building, yellow in colour and shaped like a cross with a domed centre. It does match its brief, very

Art Deco. It was built in the 1930s and designed by a Frenchman Jean Desbois, who is also responsible for a lot of the architecture and design of the city. It does explain the grid system and the wide-open boulevards that make up what is an attractive city building wise. The market itself is very cool inside, flooded with light from all the windows and slats. The inner stalls contain lots of jewellery sellers, tourist souvenirs, clothing and spices. Outside is where the more interesting and smelly stuff is going on. Food markets are all very fresh / alive in this part of the world. If your fancying spider for tea tonight, then yes, that is an option. They go out catching them in the fields around the city ready to bring to market next day. We might have been tempted – but having seen the menu earlier perhaps we will stick with the burger option tonight...

With the market ticked off our list of things to see we head further out of the city in search of what they call the Dubai Mosque (it was donated by the Arab Emirates, hence the name). We have seen pictures and it looks an attractive place, but even with map in hand we just cannot find it! After a good thirty minutes wandering around the same couple of streets blaming the map maker someone speaks enough English to explain that it had been demolished in 2014.... Not only has the Mosque gone but so has the lake, well dried up anyway.

Walking back towards base we pick up some money from the Maybank (no ATM charges) then stop for a beer in Street 51. We are a distance away from the riverfront and there is a different vibe altogether about the bars in this area. We find a Turkish bar selling beer by the jug, and offering comfortable seating, a good place to watch the world go by. The place next door seems to be a bit of a pick-up joint kind of place, a few older tourists with young locals, lots of drinks being consumed and getting friendlier with each other by the pint... Food vendors wander by, trying (and failing) to tempt us to purchase what looks like roasted sparrows, or small pigeons? Either way they look more bone than meat, hardly constitute as a proper meal. Across the road is the Heart of Darkness nightclub, it means nothing to us but that is where it all happens in this city, long past our bedtime! The beer munchies take hold as we return to our accommodation, bags of nuts and crisps will fend off the hunger until we head back out this evening.

Tonight is the first night of the 'Turning of the Tide' festival. Thousands of Cambodians descend upon the capital from their provincial hometowns to celebrate the phenomenon that is unique to here; the reversal of the waters at the confluence of the Mekong, Bassac and Tonle Sap rivers. The riverfront has really come alive and this evening the roads have become gridlocked, at least it makes crossing them a whole lot easier! As a festival, in regards to physically seeing anything then we are not blown away. At some point over the next four days, no doubt at the moons say-so, the tide will change direction. Tomorrow we are heading out of the city anyway, the countryside of Kampot beckons.

The Long Lin bar, home of the Burger, is a few streets back and away from the crowds that have descended tonight. The meal is fantastic, not a grain of rice or noodle in sight, chips that are just like chips from home. Whilst we enjoy another beer after the meal, we overhear two young English guys who from their conversation are obviously teaching out here. It seems like they are having a great life, very well paid in comparison to the living costs, lots of spare time and constant sun; and there was I thinking nothing could be worse than being a teacher!

On route back to the Blue Home Villa we treat ourselves to cocktails at the Dolphin Bar, just a dollar each. With comfortable outside seating the drinks were ok but the highlight was playing flip-flop hockey trying to keep out a large cockroach that was determined to find its way past us and into the bar.

Kampot

25th November

A new day and another bus journey. It is a seven o' clock pick up for us, a tuk-tuk collects us and just a small part of our luggage, the rest is staying here in storage until we return in a few days' time. We are soon dropped off at the large bus station that is noisy and chaotic, there are coaches everywhere and we are not one hundred percent certain which is ours. Fortunately, enough English is spoken and we are directed to the correct one.

The noise and chaos from the station barely subsides on the bus, lots of excitable children and what we now take as the obligatory blaring television playing Cambodian karaoke classics. Add lots of ants to our list of distractions. Fortunately, the noise, or at least that from the children turns down a notch or two as we leave the city confines. The motion from the bus has sent the younger ones to sleep whilst the others are engrossed in mobile phones. Before too long, (well three hours is a short journey compared to some), we pass through the small coastal town of Kep. The bay looks stunning, golden sand, blue sea and a logo featuring a giant crab proclaiming 'Welcome to Kep'. We decide that here needs investigating, and for the first time we might tweak our initial itinerary. The bus rolls on for a further twenty minutes before we reach our destination of Kampot.

Just like Battambang the bus station is on the outskirts of the town, and as before the local tuk-tuk drivers know exactly what time the buses are due to arrive. We show one of the eager drivers our booking for the NyNy Guest House, he starts at five dollars but we manage to negotiate him down to two; loading up our luggage and boarding he drives around for about five minutes, a left here, across the roundabout, left at the next, left again, another left....

Check in is smooth, this place feels more luxurious than some of the places we have stayed. Complimentary water bottles in the room and it even has the ultimate luxury experience of HOT water from the shower! With our bags dropped off we head out; reception has pointed us in the direction of the main town and river. We leave the hotel and turn left, it is no more than one hundred metres down to the roundabout where we see a supermarket, it looks familiar – no wonder... it is the one by the bus station! With our suspicions confirmed we have to laugh, twenty minutes ago we had been feeling content with our price negotiation, the tuk-tuk driver had the last laugh. Rather than point across to our accommodation he took us on a mini detour so that the journey seemed necessary and he could take a fare; fair play to him!

Kampot is a delightful place, barely any traffic on the roads and scenic river view with the Bokor mountains in the background. After spending the last few days in the bustling capital, it will be nice to take life a little easier and at a slower pace. By the river are multiple desks selling river sunset cruises to see the fireflies, so why not get one booked for this evening?

After our first hot shower in a couple of weeks we walk back down to the river and climb aboard for the river cruise. It is a fantastic way to spend our first evening, the fare includes a can of beer so with a padded cushion we sit on the floor of the upper deck and watch the sun disappear behind the mountains. As the sun goes down all the local fishing boats are returning for the evening, it really is a photographer's dream. With the sun now gone the boats pull into the side, and just as promised; hundreds of fireflies twinkling in the trees, it is like Christmas has come early. Some of our younger shipmates opt for a swim, getting off the boat is obviously easy enough, getting back on is a different matter...

26th November

The air-conditioning, along with a good bed means we have had one of our best night's sleep since we started our travels! Again, no breakfast included here so we pop next door to Jack's Café. The food is good, but then it is more expensive than most of the meals we have had, we will keep our eyes out for somewhere else for tomorrow?

We head into town and manage to hire a bike each, the cost is minimal, just a dollar each. While they may be cheap there certainly not comfortable, but the state of the roads is equally responsible for our suffering. Adjusting positions helps to alleviate the discomfort as we explore the surrounding countryside, colourful temples, small fishing villages, duck ponds, chickens and dogs! A milkshake opportunity before we cross the river and explore the other side. We even find time to have a little paddle on a sandy stretch.

After six hours are bottoms can take no more, we return the bikes and visit the two streets that make up the old market. Whilst exploring the random shops we find a bookstore and it has copies of First They Killed My Father, the book that we had been recommended when in Siem Reap. It is a true story of the horror one family went through as they fled Phnom Penh on orders of the Khymer Rouge, which is being turned into a film. We purchase a copy and add that to our ever-growing luggage. We also take the opportunity of booking a trip for tomorrow, an excellent English speaking tuk-tuk driver shows us his brochure of a village tour he offers, it looks good and having explored Kampot today our diary is free!

Back at the hotel we try to drop off our laundry, unfortunately the night staff are not as fluent in English, so that will now have to wait until the morning. Soon after that there is a power cut, the NyNy must have a generator as within a few minutes the lights are back on whilst the rest of the town remains in darkness. With the power back up we can change our travel plans and book into Kep for a couple of nights, thus reducing the number of nights we spend in Phnom Penh before heading into Vietnam.

Electricity is finally restored so we walk into Kampot in search of food. We have a couple of beers before garlic bread and pizza at the aptly named Happy Pizza restaurant. Many of the restaurants here are pizza based, and most have the word 'happy' in their name, Happy Yummy Pizza, the Happy Chef Pizza, Happy Dreams Pizza and so on. About fourteen restaurants around the town claim to make you happy, ecstatic, fun, hazy, dreamily, amazing, special...

For anyone who is not familiar with Cambodia you have probably guessed that the 'happy' come from a particular spice that is added to the pizza toppings, and no it isn't oregano! Marijuana is the 'special' ingredient that the chefs add to turn a bog-standard pizza into the happy version; be sure to ask for happy pizza upon ordering and be prepared to pay between seven and ten dollars rather than the price shown on the menu. It is highly unlikely that you will ever get arrested for eating these pizzas, but be aware that the drug laws in Cambodia are extremely strict.

27th November

Today we are meeting our driver in the old market, rather than have him pick us up from the NyNy. Laundry handed over to reception; breakfast next on the agenda! Another first on our travels - fried egg and bacon baguettes today, the options here in Kampot have improved no end - and everyone knows breakfast is not a meal to be missed!

First stop is the salt flats on the outskirts of Kampot, our driver obviously thinks we are in need of assistance as he tries to help us across a narrow bridge (it is a plank). Although his explanation of the salt flats is good it is not the time of year to see them in all their glory. Not to worry, we get the idea and enjoy watching some guy working on the irrigation system in preparation for the salt water coming in to flood the already created flats. We decline assistance walking the plank back across the ditch!

Onwards, and upwards – more bridges, plenty of awkward steps too as we make our way up to some impressive caves. When we say 'impressive' that is more for the views than the cave itself; yes, it is vast but over the years we have seen better. Our driver points out various features, tells us what they look like, but you need one hell of an imagination (or happy pizza) to see that. We nod and agree. The views are genuinely fantastic though, the Bokor mountains are the backdrop as fields, finely manicured, criss-cross all the way up to them. Alison stands in cow dung on the way back to the tuk-tuk!

Heading further into the countryside and a liquid refreshments opportunity arises. A street seller has a sugar cane press, a tarpaulin held up by sticks to give shade from the sun and some dusty plastic chairs. We watch from the chairs as she feeds the sugar cane through the press, the liquid from the press gathers in the bucket below. She then folds the crushed cane in two and repeats the procedure. Served upon ice this is like nectar, sweet and refreshing – it really quenches the thirst. She has a good spot here, other tuk-tuks pull in – as we are all on the same mission, the trip to the secret lake!

The lake appears out of nowhere, you can see why they refer to it as the secret lake, until you reach it down the dip you would have no idea it is there. What adds to the fun is that the tuk-tuks all drive through the shallow water at one end of it to come out on the other side and back up another slope that keeps it hidden from view, half-way up the slope we have visions of rolling backwards as the two-stroke engine struggles with the incline.

More countryside, villages, waving children and a multitude of farm animals before we reach the pepper plantations. We were already aware that pepper from Kampot, or at least the countryside around is regarded as the finest pepper in the world. Just like wines it is all to do with the mineral rich soil, climate (the right amount of rain and sun) and the elevation. Just like grapes for wine, several types of peppers are grown here, and just like Champagne must be from a certain region to be called that, Kampot pepper has the same PGI, Protected Geographical Indication. We wander amongst the vines and Sothy, the owner, explains of how they are farmed, protected and processed. Interestingly she tells us that the majority of Kampot pepper makes its way into the finest restaurants in Paris. As always before leaving such a place you get the hard sell of the very expensive pepper, we apologetically decline.

With our excursion completed its back into town for us, a beer and a milkshake wash down a delicious cake. We walk back towards the old market as yesterday we had seen a tour agency selling trips into the Bokor National Park; from the pictures in the folder it looks an intriguing place, abandoned buildings and beautiful scenery towards the coast on the other side of the mountains. Before returning to the NyNy we watch the fishing boats bringing back their catch, hopefully it has been a good day for them as we are planning to treat ourselves to fish and chips tonight!

After a lukewarm shower (by choice) we get dressed in to what clean clothes we have left. A fancy meal, or at least by our standards tonight; fish and chips at the Bokor Lodge restaurant. The cliental here are a little more upmarket than our regular haunts, we are sat near to a very posh couple, they are talking about going sailing. Dress wise they are immaculate, not a crease in sight... we are certain that they are paying more than a dollar per kilo for their washing! The meal was good but the service was slow and the beer was three times our usual price...

28th November

A new day and another excursion. Baguette with peanut butter is this morning's breakfast choice. As usual we are in good time and the first to arrive at the tour operator's office to wait for the minibus. The bus arrives bang-on time, as do all our fellow travellers. Just the seven of us today, two French nationals, two Dutch and the other we are not sure! Once again, we are the oldest.

Firstly, a brief history of Bokor. Most of the park is about one thousand metres above sea-level with the highest peak being Phnom Bokor at one thousand and eighty-one metres, also referred to as Bokor Mountain which in turn gives the park its name. Its history goes back almost one hundred years, originally it was a remote settlement build by the French colonialists in 1921, and incorporated a Catholic church, an exceedingly rare sight in Cambodia. The Bokor Palace hotel was first opened in 1925 by the French and was abandoned for the first time in 1946 during the Indochina war. It re-opened again in the 1960s but was abandoned again within ten years when the Bokor mountains came under control of Pol Pot's Khmer Rouge forces.

With the history of the place told we are also warned about its potential future; developments planned by the Chinese include casinos and luxury hotels – so we are pleased to be able to visit before it is destroyed, or at least changed beyond all recognition.

The winding road to the national park seems to go on and on, meandering up the hill side at a very steady pace. First stop is the Kings abandoned palace, not that it is very palatial at all. Damnak Sla Khmao (which is its full title) was built as a summer residence for King Sihanouk and was used during the fifties and sixties, before being abandoned. The building has since fallen into decay and nature has taken its hold. What you can still appreciate is the viewpoint, unobstructed lines of sight all the way to Bokor Hill. There is a more modern Buddhist pagoda, very colourful with light blue steps and a sitting Buddha perched on the top, as you get closer you appreciate just how big it is. Locals still visit here and it is considered the protector of both the mountains and the coast in this part of Cambodia.

The highlight of the trip for us is the abandoned Bokor Palace Hotel. You can wander from room to room, climb the stairs and properly explore the shell of this once great building. Although all the doors have gone there are still areas of the building that have the original flooring and tiled walls. As you work your way up to the top there are stunning views across the coast, the Gulf of Thailand. Back down to ground floor level there are vast rooms, maybe a ballroom or banqueting hall? You can imagine in the days of the 1920s how opulent this place would have been with the wealthy enjoying their stay. The fireplaces take us by surprise, this is Cambodia - the weather is hot? Our guide informs us that it can be affected by fog and damp weather at certain times of the year. The staircase, right in the centre of the building is curved and grand – perhaps leading up from the main reception? We could easily have spent another hour here, little nooks and crannies that we did not discover but time was against us.

Nearby is the Bokor church, and it does look out of place here; it is like seeing a little bit of Europe just scooped up and plonked down here in Cambodia. It is just a standard French Catholic church. There is not much to see on the inside but with it being on top of a small hill the views are spectacular.

Our dinner is provided as part of the tour, the backdrop for lunch is the rather average waterfall, nothing like the gushing water we were shown in the trip brochures – obviously the wrong time of year. Nevertheless, lunch is a tasty egg fried rice and the conversation flows between the group. This is the final part of the tour for now, one last boarding of the bus and back into town down the winding route, a whole lot quicker though than it took the driver to climb it. As we get dropped off at the office in the old market, we are advised that we need to be at the riverside for four thirty – departure time for the sunset cruise.

After a mango shake we return to the NyNy to freshen up, as we collect our key from reception we are handed our clean laundry! Its clean yet badly folded, looking crumpled has become our new normal.

The sunset cruise is an enjoyable experience, a similar route taken as to the fireflies' cruise but what is not to enjoy about watching the sun go down with a beer in your hand and chatty company? By the time we return a few bugs are being attracted to the lights, but on the plus side we do spot a kingfisher; a fitting way to end an exceptionally good tour.

29th November

Peanut butter is our new favourite breakfast. A very leisurely morning today, after two consecutive days of excursions we have nothing planned.

We wander around the old town, admiring the French architecture – generally two stories high. The post office and banks are all painted in a yellow colour and look very well kept. Maybe we have arrived a week after the painter has been? In the old town we spot a cinema, on further investigation you choose your film and rent a room with a big screen TV to view it. With nothing spoiling we opt to watch The Killing Fields, a movie truly relevant to Cambodia and one we have never seen before. Our setting to watch is a large double room with a sort of bed, come sofa to sit upon, the screen is probably at least fifty inches, so the viewing experience and sound is very good. The film ties in with a lot of what we have read and already understand about the recent history, well worth a watch.

Mango shake and a beer (creatures of habit) once we leave the 'cinema'. It all seems quiet today, not sure if it being a Sunday has any part to play, despite it being a very tourist town. Whilst having our drinks we pick up a 'Kampot News' magazine; primarily it is aimed at the English ex-pat communities who have settled in this far-flung place. An interesting read and contains an explanation of why all the roundabouts here are attractions in their own rights. The NyNy is right by the 'salt workers roundabout', but on our journey into town we pass another roundabout with a white seagull sat on top of '2000'. In the town itself is the 'Durian' roundabout and alongside the river is a globe perched on top of another. The explanation is twofold; for the tourists, an instruction referencing what is on the roundabout makes more sense than street names, and they are also visible from a good distance. For the locals it is to do with literacy, everyone recognises a seagull or globe; this explanation makes perfect sense, London Underground stations were all tiled differently for the same reasons.

One final discovery on our route back to our digs, we discover the Kampot pond. It is marked on the maps as a place to visit, so why not. With a little imagination it could be a lovely place, and it may well be before too long – by the amount of machinery, shovels and trenches that have been dug it looks like it is being refurbished.

Evenings in Kampot are low key, we eat at our usual place and enjoy a beer or several before heading in for an early night. What we have come to realise is that for a lot of these small restaurants and bar establishments the toilet facilities are the family bathroom; toothbrushes are often in the glass by the sink, dressing gown hanging on the back of the door...

Kep

30th November

Today is 'moving day', but for us no karaoke on the bus, Kep is near enough to reach by tuk-tuk!

Having checked out of the NyNy we sit on the steps waiting for our driver, in no time he arrives but with two other passengers who are also heading that way. He asks if we mind, not a problem to us. The two girls are from Somerset on the south coast of England so we have a good chat and we all share experiences, seems that we are all loving Cambodia! Before we know it, we are approaching the outskirts of Kep and we spot the sign for our accommodation, the Bird of Paradise Bungalows. We unfasten our luggage, say our goodbyes, and head up a dusty path following the sign.

Turning into the gates we are blown away; we knew it looked nice when we booked it on our phones – this is better than we imagined. The bungalows are wooden huts on stilts, straw roofs and with individual verandas, complete with hammocks! Landscaped gardens, ducks and a cat all add to the instant attraction of the place. The Aussie owner is very friendly and takes us to our 'hut'. Over a welcome drink Peter, our Aussie host points in various directions. To the end of the drive, turn left and then right to the sea, left and straight on for the town and if you want to head up to the mountain that we are at the foot of turn right out the gate. That covers everything, Kep really is that small, although scattered around the mountain area there are abandoned homes from the 1960s, left to rot and be swallowed up by nature.

We head down towards the sea, (it really is just a five-minute walk away); a pair of grand hotels on the route down, with uniformed staff at the gates – even if we had plenty of money and a bigger budget, we would not swap our wooden hut experience for a standard hotel room. The crab market is at the bottom of the hill, stall after stall selling crabs, as you can guess the smell is overpowering. Locals are buying crabs and they cannot be any fresher, the ladies selling them wade out to the pots to retrieve the crabs for each order. Turning left beyond the market are all the restaurants, every menu option looks fish based, and every menu looks a lot more expensive than what we have become used to!

We leave the restaurants behind and continue walking around the headland, monkeys are wandering in the road and emptying the bins opposite, scavenging for food. Once we are beyond the peninsula the beach appears, lovely golden sand and crystal-clear waters, that is us sorted for tomorrow. Away from the beach is the small-town centre, and despite only just having arrived we book a bus for a couple of days' time back to Phnom Penh.

Returning to the Bird of Paradise we sit and melt on the veranda for a little while, the hammock is more of a novelty – getting in and out needs to be practised on, but once settled it is surprisingly stable. The gardens are very colourful, and do have the Bird of Paradise flower from which the accommodation takes its name. If we were surprised at how comfortable the hammocks were, we are shocked when we shower, hot water again!

With the sun setting we make our way to the seafront to watch the world go by. I get some fantastic photographs of fishing boats sailing through the reddish, orange reflection on the water, crab pots glistening. Hungry now, we pace up and down checking the menus, in the end we opt for a place purely because it was busy. Banana chips / crisps are brought to our table to nibble on whilst we decide what to order. We really should try the crab but upon seeing other people struggling with the nutcrackers and knifes we are convinced they look more trouble than their worth. Effort versus reward, unless you are a professional, looks very weighted in favour of effort. We both enjoy seafood, so we order the lime and chilli squid served with sticky rice. It turns out to be one of the best meals we have eaten, so we do not even begrudge the bill being triple that of our regular evening meal! They had given us fresh juicy pineapple too; we will count that as a pudding...

Back at the bungalows we enjoy a beer or two with Peter and another guest, he's Swiss but his English is perfect. We also discover that the cat is called Coco. The beer or two turns into four or five before a thunderstorm breaks out, we are soaked before we make it back to our room. The bed is firm, how we like it and with a mosquito net hanging above, the room is cool and in pitch darkness, the only noise is from the still rumbling thunder...

1st December

We wake early, not sure if that has been brought about by the wildlife noises from outside or our headaches from the aptly named 6% Clang beer. We manage a little more sleep before getting up for breakfast. With immediate need for coffee its fortunate that breakfast options are available here, though not included in the room rate. Toasted baguette and fresh fruit settle any remaining hangover symptoms. That thunderstorm last night may well have saved today from being a write-off...

Today is the first opportunity we have had to head to the beach, so we take a book, towels and sun tan lotion and make the ten-minute walk. The beach is almost our own private facility, there are very few people about. We do have a little swim but after seeing a handful of jellyfish we are easily put off, never mind, laying on the beach is not a bad second choice. After a couple of hours that is enough for us, as much as we like the idea of a lazy day on the beach the reality is we get bored too easily!

Even after showering we have the whole afternoon still ahead of us, so we borrow a pair of bikes from Peter and head off to explore. It does not take us long to conclude that Kep is a strange place; beyond the initial town area we follow the coast road, just the odd hotel and lots of hammock hire places. If you go a road further back from here, they are wide and new, but with hardly any purpose to them – they don't really lead to anywhere and nothing much is built on them bar the odd government building. By this point we are ridiculously hot and thirsty, desperate for water but a long way from anywhere!

Eventually we find someone with a cool box selling ice-cold water, and with our thirst quenched we head up towards the mountains, often having to get off and walk. Coming back down will be far easier! It does not take us long to discover some of Kep's abandoned buildings, they look like in their prime they would have been lovely villas, plots in prime positions that gave them amazing views down to the coastline. What puzzles us is why no one has ever reclaimed them once Cambodia had returned to normal? Two hours cycling in this heat has us beat, we feel we see as much as we were going too without knocking ourselves out. Back in town we have a beer and get chatting to a guy, and once he discovers that we are soon heading to Ho Chi Minh City and have been there once before he is full of questions. Its normally us full of questions, so good to have been of use to someone else in return!

Showered and changed its sunset time again; a well-earned cold beer to watch the sun drop into the ocean before ordering food. This evening we are sat in the Crab Kitchen and on their very crabby menu is crab noodles and crab fried rice, having seen someone else order this we realise that this dish avoids the nutcrackers, claw breaking and all that faff that puts us off the hard-shelled creature. The crab was sparse, more infused with shavings than chunky bits of meat, we wouldn't write home about it; but at least we gave it a go!

As we return to the Bird of Paradise Bungalows, we can hear thunder rumbling in the background, it comes to nothing so we sit out and have another chat with Peter our host, but drink a few less Clangs than last night. Tomorrow we are on the move back to Phnom Penh.

Tonights big shock is the size of the spider nestling in the toilet bowl...

Return to Phnom Penh

2nd December

At 4 a.m. Alison goes the toilet, somehow the spider has reappeared, it is obviously a good swimmer (or maybe a different spider?). It has been another good nights sleep, we will be sad in some ways to leave here, a cool room, hot water, pretty gardens and an amiable host – it has the lot.

Scrambled eggs and pancakes are our breakfasts this morning, and with that eaten we have one last walk down to the crab market and beach before returning to pack our bags and check out. Upon leaving we have one last beer and spend some time chatting to an Aussie couple, they have already been Vietnam and have had an amazing time, we are now quite looking forward to that part of our journey, better food options being the main reason!

The mini-bus picks us up, and we are expecting that to take us to a larger bus for the journey; that is not the case and within three hours we are back in Phnom Penh. The journey was ok as the mini-bus was only half full, the driver was quick but not reckless, so not too much gripping of the seats! As we can see the bright yellow Central Market we know exactly where we are so set off on foot back to the Blue Home Villa. Our hosts are pleased to see us back, we are given a very warm welcome – and even better than that, we have a bigger room and a fan – things are on the up!

Planning for our departure appears to be a constant theme, we drop in our laundry to make sure it is returned to us in plenty of time before we move on to Vietnam. We also ask our hosts about arranging our bus tickets, they say they will make some calls and let us know a price.

Very traditional food tonight, even if the restaurant does not have an authentic Cambodian name; we are back in the Pink Elephant where we order a beef lok lak and chicken with cashew nuts. With our meal finished we move on to the Blue Dolphin for Mojitos, the location of the previous skirmish with a cockroach. No 'roach' action tonight so we have to settle for a rat wandering by instead! By 10 p.m. we are done for, back to the Blue Home Villa and a hot sticky room, so much for that fan...

3rd December

Wooden huts are the way forward, so much cooler to sleep in! A disturbed night sleep is the only way to describe it.

Long Lin again for breakfast, beans on toast... We walk beyond the Central Market to the Maybank ATM, more money required. I am desperately in need of new shoes, well flip-flops / sandals, but like most men hate shopping. Seeing that we are so close to the market we do make a half-hearted search for some replacements. After thirty minutes or so we lose the will, all seem to be either plastic and ridiculously cheap or expensive, more than you would pay at home anyway.

It is as we are heading towards the river that Alison spots a shoe repair guy working by the side of the road. For two dollars he glues and stitches the front of my sandals, chuffed as anything they look as good as new! Continuing towards the river and we are stopped from crossing the road by the Police, we are not sure why or what is going on but within a minute or two there is a big cavalcade of cars with important looking people sat in them all led and followed by armed police cars. Once they have passed, he cheerily waves us across and on our way – who they were will remain a mystery.

At the river we suss out boat trips, we have a few days left in Phnom Penh and time to fill... With it being so hot, what better way to pass the time than with a jug of beer and watch the world go by (again). Looking at the time we know that we cannot get into the Royal Palace until after two o' clock so we head back to base. Our smiley host has only gone and upgraded our fan to a big free-standing, oscillating one, hopefully that will make for a better sleep tonight?

We take the alternative route to the Palace, around the less glamorous back than the photogenic front and happen to find a man with a trolley selling iced coffees. In the glaring heat of the day this is just what we need, and reasonably priced too, compared to the over-inflated prices of the vendors at the front.

The Royal Palace itself is well worth the entry fee, whilst its impressive it is nothing like on the scale of the Grand Palance in Bangkok but it is still a stunning piece of architecture. The colours are bright, and with the sun beating down the whole complex sparkles and glistens. Although there is some signage around the place, detailing what each building is, it is not too 'heavy' on details like names and dates. The Throne Hall and Moonlight Pavilion are our favourite parts of the site. The Silver Pagoda is different, but with it being the home to many national treasures entry inside is not permitted. All in all, we spend about two hours wandering around the complex, with it not being overly busy it is a pleasant way to pass the afternoon.

More sugar cane drinks as we head back to the river for our boat trip. With the boat only half full it sets off, just a gentle cruise up to the confluence of where the river Mekong and the Tonle Sap join, directly opposite the Royal Palace. There are plenty of little fishing boats dotted around and a fishing village right on the junction of where the two rivers meet. It also gives us an alternative view of Phnom Penh that is now lighting up as dusk falls.

Our evening follows the same pattern as most others, shower, a couple of beers, seek out food; and ever since we discovered the Blue Dolphin, Mojitos have been added to the nightly ritual. No cockroaches or rats this evening, instead entertainment comes from a 'Mr Bean' type character, smirking and gesturing to himself!

4th December

The fan does its job, or at least after a strategic change of position! We changed in the middle of the night and sleep with our pillows at the foot end of the bed rather than the usual way around. For some reason the centre of the room seems to be cooler than the wall end...

With shoes repaired yesterday the opportunity for some male grooming arises today. Street barber, complete with a mirror hung on a tree and a proper pair of scissors – the Cambodian equivalent of Vidal Sassoon. To be fair he does a terrific job (there is not a lot to work with), plus I also get eyebrows trimmed and a shoulder massage thrown in. The price is a bargain at two dollars.

The National Museum of Cambodia passes away another hour or two, there are some really impressive relics, parts of bigger carvings that look amazing. Other 'relics' look like bits of stone fresh from any one of the numerous building sites around the city. The labelling of the exhibits is vague - date, location but not really elaborating any more than that. On the positive side there was a lovely central garden with a pond. The best bit about giving these places a go is that even if they are not your cup of tea the entry cost is minimal.

Over a beer we get chatting to (another) Aussie guy, he splits his time between Phnom Penh and Ho Chi MInh City – exporting Kampot pepper to Japan. We are soon back on our way and heading to the Central Market area, or more specifically the jewellers around it; as well as selling shiny things they are also the best places to change currency. With us heading to Vietnam tomorrow now seems to be the perfect time to convert some of our American dollars into Vietnamese dong.

Back at base our laundry has appeared in reception, we settle our bill for that and the onward bus journey to HCMC (Ho Chi Minh City) and rearrange our luggage. With an early start tomorrow, we wander along the riverside for one last time, watching the local's playing badminton, doing yoga, having picnics... Nothing adventurous food wise, burgers at the Long Lin, one Mojito at the Blue Dolphin and back home for a good night's sleep.

Top row: Pub Street, Siem Reap; Bamboo train and the Lok Ta Dumbong roundabout, Battambang

Middle: Bayon Temple, Angkor Thom and Angkor Wat

Bottom: Skulls at the Choeung Ek Killing Field and Kep by day and sunset

Cambodia Observations...

Such friendly, happy people – determined that the past is not going to stop them from enjoying the future.

Why park on the road when there is a place on the path available?

Meals ordered together very rarely get served at the same time.

Currency keeps you on your toes, pay in dollars, receive change in riels or sometimes a mix of the two!

It is exceedingly rare to see older Cambodians wearing glasses, does that go back to the Pol Pot era where that alone would be enough to have you classed as educated, and put to death?

Ladies wear pyjamas to go shopping, and that applies whatever the time of day.

They also wear gloves in thirty-degree heat...

So many amputees begging, sadly there is no government help or assistance for the disabled.

They love a picnic by the Mekong River or Royal Palace! Each evening they bring out their mats; no pavement is spared.

Hammocks! Another Cambodian passion, they can be hired like we would a deckchair in days gone by.

No minimum age to ride a scooter, well unless it is as low as seven years old!

Hot showers very rarely exist...

Scooters fit the whole family, be that a family of four, five and sometimes even the dog.

Building sites are everywhere, we have never seen a country developing so quickly.

Restaurants all have identical menus throughout the country, only the price varies.

Early mornings and again in the evenings, any free space turns into a pop-up sports venue, spontaneous yoga breaks out everywhere.

Paper napkins on every restaurant table are all perfumed.

Choice of cars seems limited to 4 x 4s, usually the Lexus.

Anyone holding a TEFL qualification can be an English teacher in Cambodia.

Durian is banned in more places than guns and drugs, that must be one stinky fruit.

Ho Chi Minh City, Vietnam

5th December

We both slept well, there is method not madness in changing our sleeping position! We say goodbye to our hosts and leave by tuk-tuk to get our bus. We have just enough riels left to purchase baguettes and crisps for the journey.

The bus is very comfortable, the best one yet – reclining seats, foot rests and lots of leg room – or maybe us being short helps on that front. A very mixed bunch on this bus, for once tourists look to outnumber the locals; and unusually we are not the oldest. The journey to the Cambodia : Vietnam border is uneventful. The area approaching the Cambodian border is full of luxury hotels and casinos, a strange sight and not in keeping with the rest of the country. Duty Free shops and toilet facilities are also available where the bus drops us off for refreshments.

Upon reaching the border we must vacate the bus once more, this time with our luggage. Still on the Cambodian side, we pass through their immigration and get our visas checked (we haven't overstayed), and then our visa stamped. Goodbye Cambodia! Leaving the immigration hall what can only be described as an uninhabited land of fifty metres or so before we reach the Vietnamese immigration office. Passports out again, visa inspected and passport stamped. Luggage is to be scanned next, we join the queue at the scanning machine and put our bag on the belt, they pass through the x-ray machine and we collect at the other end. Bizarrely no one is even sat at the x-ray machine!

There is a little bit of waiting around before the bus arrives for us all to board again, presumably it must have been searched too? With everyone accounted for Ho Chi Minh City (HCMC) here we come. As we approach the city, we recognise some of the landmarks, it is only eight months since we were last here, a mere fortnights holiday in the days when we had jobs... To make our start in HCMC easier we have even booked into the hotel that we stayed in last April, and when the bus drops us off, we know exactly where we are. It is just a fifteen-minute walk to the Tulips Hotel; we receive a friendly welcome as the Vietnamese couple who run it remember us from our previous visit. We get checked in, and even have the same room as last time, for the first time since Bangkok we have proper facilities and can hang some clothes up. Our room, although still in the budget bracket is a step up from Cambodian standards, hot water, air-conditioning, even a fridge! Breakfast seems to be included as standard in our Vietnamese bookings, though it is nice to eat out each morning it can be inconvenient, and it can work out expensive, or at least in budget travel terms.

We walk to a bar we used regular, right on the corner of De Tham street, the backpackers quarter; prices are still soooo cheap! Faces of the couple at the table nearby look familiar, we get talking, their Canadian, and yes, they were in Kampot at the same time as us. Not a case of 'small world' more that tourists are following a fairly standard route exploring these two countries. It turns out that they travel for six months every year, avoiding their icily cold winters that would make ours seem positively tropical! They are more adventurous than us, no set plans – just making it up as they go along!

Our first evening meal in HCMC is a very local affair, spring rolls and noodle soup. Although we have been here before it takes a little while to become accustomed to the sheer amount of traffic, ninety-nine percent of which is made up of scooters!

6th December

The comfort of our top floor room has given us a good night's sleep. With nothing specific on our agenda today it is a leisurely breakfast; my fried rice was a little on the dry side, Alison had opted for the scrambled egg, and it arrived with two large rolls, butter and jam – undoubtedly the better choice of the two.

Yesterday had been an inactive day spent travelling, so we opt to walk out to the Le Van Duyet Temple. Although we can see it the gate to get in takes a little finding! The temple itself is a shrine to a General of the same name who helped reunify Vietnam in the early nineteenth century. We are not too big on the history side, too many names and dates but can appreciate the temple for its colour and displays. Our stay takes a lot longer than intended as Alison starts to feel unwell, so we spend a lot of time sitting in the grounds hoping the shade and taking on of fluids will help her recover.

After a while we do start walking back before a further relapse means a taxi is the best option. On the plus side it has taken until the fortieth day of travelling before either of us have succumbed to illness! With the help of a cool room, rest and plenty more water some level of normality is restored, though not enough to fancy any food this evening - most unusual!

As a lone man heading out for food I do survive, being on your own you do get hassled more by street sellers, and I do not just mean by those selling bangles...

7th December

A solid breakfast of eggs, bread rolls and a couple of cups of strong coffee ensure normal health and fitness has been restored.

A wandering, walking tour and we will see where it takes us. Early on we take in a Hindu temple only a few streets away from where we are staying, from our travels around India over the last ten years we recognise many of the idols represented in the displays. Although not religious at all we do like to take in these places, such colourful buildings, the smell of incense sticks and offerings; and they are most definitely a place of serenity, an oasis of calm amongst the chaos of the busy streets.

More familiar sights from the guidebook are soon upon us; the Notre-Dame Cathedral Basilica of Saigon, or its official title 'Cathedral Basilica of Our Lady of The Immaculate Conception'. Not surprisingly it looks remarkably like a French church of the same name... Crossing the road from the cathedral and you are at what is possibly the worlds grandest post office. It is referred to as the Central Post Office and, courtesy of Google, it is of gothic, renaissance, and French influence; constructed between 1886 and 1891 but despite what many are led to believe it was not the work of Gustave Eiffel of tower fame. Either way it is a very impressive building even if it is merely a tourist attraction these days.

With referring to the cathedral as 'of Saigon' now is a good opportunity to bring up the Ho Chi Minh City versus Saigon name... Saigon is the old name of Ho Chi Minh City; the change was made in April 1975 when the city was captured by the North Vietnamese troops who promptly renamed it in honour of their revolutionary leader. Which is correct today? It does seem like the answer is either, the airport code is SGN but your ticket refers to it as HCMC. Officially it is Ho Chi Minh City, but it is very interchangeable and neither cause offence; just for consistency I will use its abbreviated name, HCMC!

We spot a couple of museums, but with the weather so nice we walk by, an option if we get a rainy day? By the riverside we watch a cruise ship docking, no doubt ready to march tourists around the city on a whistle-stop tour and tick off Vietnam as having been visited! An iced coffee break, and a divine one too, the quantity of condensed milk that went into that, it is certainly not a diet option! Coffee in Vietnam is that good that on our last visit in April we took home packs of the stuff, rather than the more traditional duty-free drinks.

A walk around the market turns out to be less stressful than anticipated, not too much hassle from the stallholders who have the unbelievable knack of knowing exactly what has grabbed your attention. Even if you have not picked anything up, they just know! Short of being a mind reader they must instead have an incredible talent for watching your every eye movement, quickly grabbing it from their display, trying to tempt you... There are plenty of potential purchases, but room is limited.

Heading back to the Tulips hotel via De Tham street gives us the chance not only for a couple of beers (at twenty-five pence each why not), but also to look at the bus timetable to Can Tho on the Mekong delta. We spent a nightmare few hours in Can Tho on our previous visit, this time we hope for a better experience, but before that a few more days here. On our return to the hotel, we pick up our clean laundry, very efficient as we had only dropped it off this morning. One bonus addition, as we unpack our clean washing we have a bonus item of a pink thong, far too small for either of us!

Showered and fresh we retrace much of our route today, enjoying seeing the city lit up, getting ready for Christmas Vietnamese style. Food wise, it is a safe option, pizza and garlic bread.

8th December

A loud bang at 3 a.m. disturbs us; but not for long – another night of quality sleep. Downstairs to the foyer for a breakfast of fried noodles.

Heading out beyond the cathedral and post office we eventually reach the Jade Emperor Pagoda, which is also known as the Tortoise Pagoda. Today must be their bath day, the pond that they inhabit has been drained right down and is having a power wash, we are unable to decide if they are enjoying the experience or not, they do keep wandering to where the jet is hitting before the flow of water coming back from the wall pushes them back. It is an amusing way to spend some time! The pagoda itself is not as elaborate as some, this one being a Taoist temple, but the gardens are a lovely setting in which to have a chill for a while.

Departing from here we reach the canal, a perfect opportunity to have an iced coffee at a local café. We are treat like royalty as some young lads give up their chairs for us. They are keen to chat, no doubt to practise their English, but they also teach us a few Vietnamese words to help us in ordering our drinks. They all leave on mass, perhaps heading to a local school or college? Continuing our walk along the side of the canal brings us to the Vinh Nghiem Pagoda, very picturesque, but just like the other day we again struggle to find the entrance. Despite being a pagoda this one is Buddhist, but relatively new. Seven stories high and the first in the city to be made in the Vietnamese traditional architecture style, unusually it is constructed entirely from concrete. We pop into a third temple on our way back towards District 1; colourful as it was it did not merit a mention in our guide book.

Our afternoon is spent in the Independence Palace, or at least once we have made our way past the army of shoe-shiners outside the gate, maybe shiny shoes or sandals are a condition of entry? Nowadays it is just a tourist attraction, but in its not-too-distant past it had been the home and workplace of the President of South Vietnam. Historically it is most famous from the image of a tank bursting through the gates as Saigon fell on the thirtieth of April 1975, and with that the ending of the Vietnam war.

It is not the most attractive building externally, wide and squat. The grounds in front contain a few military items; tanks, planes, helicopters and the like, a big fountain in the lake is the centrepiece. The rooms inside have been refurbished (taken back?) to how they would have been in the 1970s at the time of conflict. Some rooms are in the manner of a stately home, whilst others are purely functional and obviously war related with the maps and markings of who is fighting and controlling where. Of course, up on the roof is the spot where the last American helicopters fled from, and their take on the ending of the 'American War' as they flee.

Whilst cooling off in our room we discover Saigon Zoo, the reviews of it are a bit mixed, but that is quite normal, they do tend to divide opinion. In the ideal world animals would be in their natural habitat, but if zoos help people understand, and learn about the damage we are doing to them and their environment, then is that an argument for their good?

Before heading for food, we saunter around the night market, it is the same stuff as in the day but not so well lit. After sheltering from a brief thunderstorm, we eventually get to eat; the clay pot pork dish was delicious, the chicken and cashew more a game of hunt the cashew! Fortunately, the fresh spring rolls and the dipping sauce we had as starters meant we did not leave either hungry or disappointed.

9th December

Noodles for breakfast, the second day running.

It has been a while since we had a 'grim' day; the War Remnants Museum will bring an end to that. It was originally known as the 'Exhibition House for U.S. and Puppet Crimes', then changed to 'Exhibition House for Crimes and Aggression'. Over the years, as the relationship with America has thawed and improved the museum name has been toned down accordingly.

Outside the museum, just like at the Independence Palace there are a selection of aircraft and tanks, some captured American ones, many of their own. Along with the museums name is a white dove logo, representing peace that has finally been restored after thirty years of turmoil, first with the French and then the more familiar battle with the Americans. In Vietnam they never refer to it as the Vietnam war, it is the opposite to them, the American war.

Inside the museum are harrowing stories going back all the way from seeking independence from France in the 1940s, through to 1975 when the country becomes reunited. With a mixture of photographs and exhibits it tells the story of the horrors that beset the country in those years. Among the grizzlier pieces are jars of deformed foetuses from expectant mothers who had been exposed to dioxins. Agent Orange, a chemical that the Americans sprayed over vast areas of the country is still having an impact today. Birth defects and forms of cancer are still being linked to its use, both among the Vietnamese but also US military veterans. Areas of the country have still been unable to be reforested forty years on. Agent Orange and the heavily used cluster bombs are fortunately weapons that (hopefully) would never be used today.

It was an interesting two plus hours, more so to hear the story from a second viewpoint rather than the familiar one portrayed in American films. A tour group pass through whilst we were in there, rudely pushing through behind their guide; he obviously has a tight schedule, look at this – move on; but what can you learn at such a breakneck speed?

Back outside we discover a Catholic church with an interesting shrine outside. With no signage at all we can only assume that all the plaques with names on are deceased, and that is their equivalent of a gravestone? Either way, it is a very pretty memorial garden, even if the church is bright pink. At our regular late afternoon bar are the Canadian couple, savouring their last few hours hour before heading off for Laos, we wish them well – another place that is on our 'to do' list. Back home to freshen up and contemplate what we are having for tea!

Evening meals are getting more exotic, a mango and pork salad and a beef noodle with cashew nuts. The remainder of the evening is spent on little plastic chairs drinking gin by the jar. A fantastic place for people watching, jugglers and fire eaters to the front.... local teenagers eating chicken's feet behind...

10th December

Both feeling a little tender this morning, we overdid the gin. Noodle breakfast, now a staple part of our diet. An extra black coffee before normal service is resumed.

We set off on foot towards the zoo, a longer walk than we estimated but interesting nonetheless. The road leading up towards the zoo seems to have a lot of countries Embassy offices, grand buildings behind high fences with security on the gates, the road also seems to go on and on forever.

The zoo is far better (and bigger) than we expected. Even after being there for three hours, we were still discovering new parts. The big cats were as impressive as always, or at least when they were awake. The usual selection of large animals, elephants, hippos, giraffes – but so strange to see them with a backdrop of skyscrapers. We could not get the image out of our head of living on the third floor and a giraffe staring through your window!

The orangutans had a nice enclosure, good in size and plenty to amuse them, some of the other monkeys were not so fortunate though, their cages barely looked big enough. The collection of snakes was as good as we have ever seen, quite terrifying of just how big they can grow! We even spoil ourselves with an ice cream, and are surprised that it is no more expensive than on the streets outside; so different to back home where you either pay extortionate prices or go without.

For what it is worth we thought the zoo was on a par with conditions that we have seen in the UK, some of the bad reviews that we had read did not tie in with what we had seen. While we had been a little undecided in should we visit or not we were able to return into the city pleasantly surprised having really enjoyed a different type of day - well worth the Dong equivalent of one pound fifty! Keeping with the animal theme, on our way back we see a guy on a motorbike who was selling tropical fish by the roadside. A rack on the back of his bike had a dozen or more bags, like you see at the fairground, very innovative of him.

By the time we have got back we have been on our feet for a solid seven hours, a lay down and rest before we venture out this evening. When we do return out, we treat ourselves to an Indian meal, we feel spoilt as it has proper full-sized chairs and tablecloths, proper posh! The curry was better than we dared hope for, so with our stomachs full we now do head back to the tiny plastic chairs for drinks.

The ladies who run these street bars are not to be messed with, there is not much choosing where you sit, she tells you, shouting to get your attention and pointing to where you should be... With it just being the two of us there is no way you can sit at a group table, fortunately we have seen others shouted at on previous nights and escape her wrath. For the third night running Alison has been chatting with a little lady who sells chewing gum, she is so friendly with a massive smile, it is impossible to turn her down! Three drinks later (no jars tonight) we return to base.

11th December

After yet another noodle breakfast we head off to Ben Thanh market, it is another iconic building of the city, over one hundred years old and like the post office it is from the French colonial era. Whilst it has been renovated multiple times over the last century it retains the original shape, and hence the character that makes it a favourite of tourists looking for holiday souvenirs.

We manage to buy some T-shirts; it should be an easy task but with so many stalls and shirt designs it is a mind-blowing experience – too much choice! The handbag search is an epic failure, try again tonight? Outside of the inner sanctum is the 'wet' market, it is here where you can buy almost anything, or at least it seems that way to us. Turtles, terrapins, frogs, fish, dead or alive – a fascinating place and so vibrant to what we are used to back home.

Today is going to be a lazy day, we return our shopping back to the room and have a quick surf, check out a few options for things to do tomorrow. Arranging bus tickets is our number one priority for this afternoon, the Futa Bus booking office is only a five-minute walk away, right in the heart of the backpacker district. After the miles we covered yesterday rest is today's plan, luckily our favourite daytime bar is near enough, and has soft seats.

The Futa office is chaotic, but we are in no rush and are feeling relaxed, maybe due to the iced coffee that we have just enjoyed on route! We get our tickets, wrongly we had assumed that all Futa buses depart from the booking office but that is not the case, the bus to Can Tho leaves from elsewhere in the south of the city, not a problem that a short taxi journey will not solve.

Our usual bar is unusually busy, so we cross the road and sit in the one directly opposite, and the beer is ice cold, shame we never discovered here earlier. Our position is situated right on a 'T' junction, a front row seat and the perfect position to people watch and while away two or three hours. The number of street vendors in the day is even more than by night, although they are selling different goods. Daytime its brushes, bread, fruit – more aimed at the locals, by night its cigarettes, watches, laughing gas, squashed squid and chicken's feet.

We do go home for a freshen up, a game or three of scrabble and a little sleep before we return to De Tham street to enjoy our evening. Our second lot of noodles for the day plus spring roll starters sets us up before we go for a couple of drinks. Plastic chairs and gin by the jar are probably where we go wrong, the evening is fantastic and we are laughing at people who are buying the laughing gas and speaking in that strange way after. Vendors inflate balloons with it, you then inhale by letting the air out into your mouth, you cannot help but smile and laugh.

While we feel fine walking home in the night heat, it is when we get into our cool air-conditioned room that the drunk feeling kicks in. It is the opposite way round from at home; you leave the warm pub and the chilly air hits you once you get outside!

12th December

We both wake up feeling rubbish, but at least I manage to rise for breakfast. Alison stays in bed feeling sorry for herself!

By late morning we venture out, Alison doing the walk of shame through reception; I had let slip that she was missing breakfast due to over indulging in the gin. Our mission; the Ho Chi Minh Museum – the revolutionary leader not the city itself. It does involve quite a walk as it is down by the river. As we arrive it is still shut for lunch, so a fifteen-minute spell wandering around the outside of it, a few plaques to read, a sit on a wall soon pass that time.

The museum was average at best, very heavy on the reading front though. By the time we leave I guess we have more of an understanding of his ideals, but it is extremely complicated – and very biased. It is a strange museum, just the two floors high but crammed with photographs. Most interesting, for us at least, was seeing the pictures from the 1950s of buildings and places we have visited; the contrast in how the city has maintained these old buildings alongside the new skyline of skyscrapers is admirable. At the time of the photos the Cathedral, post office, Ben Thanh market etc. all dwarf their surroundings – how times have changed.

Returning to the heart of the city we plan to visit the Central Mosque. Somehow, we have never seen it, despite its proximity to the Opera house and City Hall - it has persistently eluded us. With map in hand, we wander around a pair of side streets, almost doubling back on ourselves and there it is; it is a stunning white building with mint green trim, but dwarfed by huge hotels that have been built all around it, penning it in. Whilst the hotels are all neatly parallel to the roads grid system, the Mosque is at a jaunty angle, obviously the first to be built and facing Mecca.

Jamia Al Muslimin Mosque, to use its full title, was built in the 1930s by Muslim expatriates from South India, this makes it the first mosque in what was then Saigon. We were happy to admire it from outside the gates, but someone visiting it for prayer encouraged us to borrow the gowns put aside for visitors and take a closer look. Taking him up on the offer we venture through the gates and admire the architecture and intricate design features, we are made to feel very welcome as he points out the various rooms within.

Feeling peckish we find a nearby bakery and enjoy some pastries as a late afternoon snack. Looking down at my already repaired once sandals I begin to doubt if they will survive all the way to Goa. With one eye out for shoe shops or market stalls we return to the Tulips.

Once again, we shun noodles and rice this evening, opting for a homemade burger at the Bookworms Café. Saturday night and its heaving, all the locals are out enjoying their weekend alongside the tourists, but for us an early night, tomorrow we are back on the move. Smiley chewing gum lady has expanded her stock tonight, how can we resist buying a bangle or two from her on our final night?

Can Tho

13th December

Well, it has been a fantastic stay at the Tulips, and the final breakfast sends us on our way to Can Tho with full stomachs (even if I got fried rice despite ordering noodles!). We say goodbye to our hosts for the second time this year and head outside to hail a taxi; not just any taxi, we will only use a Vinasun or Mai Linh as we have been advised that these are both reliable and metered.

Safely delivered to the Futa offices (we were expecting a bus station) and it is not long before we are boarded onto a minibus and offloaded on a wide street further out, on the outskirts of the city, still no bus station in sight! We need not have worried, the big orange Futa bus soon arrives and a handful of us board the already half full bus. First impressions are very good; well-padded seats, and no karaoke! There is a TV but it does appear to have a volume control button, Cambodian versions only have the one setting, full blast. It looks to be showing some type of variety show but no one is paying it any attention, phones and headsets the order of the day.

With a journey time of around three and a half hours we are afforded one toilet break. It is good to get off as while the seats are comfortable, they are also sweaty! We take the opportunity to buy lollies, although Alison wears most of hers as she is beaten in the race to eat it before it melts. Overall though it is a good journey and we arrive close to our scheduled arrival time. We are lucky that someone told us that Futa bus fares include a shuttle bus to hotels within the city – so with that in mind we fend off the throng of taxi drivers looking for fares.

In no time we have been dropped off by the shuttle bus at the Hau Giang 2 hotel. A quick check in and with keys in hand we head to our room, small but functional is a good description of it. Hot water again, that is still one of our first checks whenever we change accommodation.

Our last visit to Can Tho in April was a disaster, so bad that you could not make it up. It started with the bus breaking down, and then the driver getting lost. It got worse; we were sold our Mekong trip on the basis that it was finished by midday (we had a flight to catch), once on the river trip we were advised that was not the case it would be 1pm before our return. The Can Tho part of that holiday was just stressful, although we did manage to catch our flight! This time we have a few days to explore so no such worries lie ahead.

Arriving early afternoon means that exploring in daylight hours is easily done, we soon discover that we are very central, just the one street back from the vast Mekong River. We are also close to where the nightly food market is held and discover a few agencies selling tours of the river, everything we need is right on our doorstep.

By night we explore our way around the food market, one lap first before committing to anything, second lap choosing the best of what we have seen. A local rice paper style pancake snack is our choice, very tasty, and although tempted by other options we have a local restaurant earmarked for food later. A plastic glass of sugar cane juice washes that down before we head away from the river into the confines of the town.

Upon finding the restaurant it was not how we imagined, open-sided with stainless steel tables, none of the usual plastic menus but instead huge pictures on the wall of the food options; not a word is written in English. We choose three random meals, not really knowing what they are, by pointing at them and are taken to the fridges to select our drinks. The food is fantastic, different textures, sweet and sour – we have struck gold with discovering this place on our first night. We had a crispy noodle dish with chicken, rice with pork and a tray of rice pancakes, sausage of some kind and lots of leaves (none that we recognised). By watching other tables, we figure out that you lay the leaves on the pancakes and then add the sausage and roll. The spicy dipping sauce just added to the flavour and we ploughed our way through them, even eating all the leaves! The bill comes to fifty thousand dong, so just a shade over one pound fifty for a meal and drink that has left us both stuffed...

Like Battambang, Can Tho seems low key in the evenings, although as we get back to the riverside, we do find a handful of bars and restaurants where the tourists and teachers are enjoying a beer or two. Teachers are a constant on our travels, so many are over here with the TEFL (Teaching English as a Foreign Language) qualification, perhaps the constant pleasant weather, work / life balance and cheap beer is the attraction...

14th December

We both sleep well and are excited about our first breakfast at our latest hotel. Buffet style for the first time, but unfortunately not the most exciting spread. Peanut butter is our go to option, it does exactly what it says on the jar, and on the positive side a bonus of iced coffee! With the breakfast room being right at the top of the building as well as working up an appetite getting there, we also get some good panoramic views across the city.

A proper explore is today's mission, yesterday's walk only covered the essentials, food and tour booking options. There are a few more temples and pagodas scattered across the city to take in, the Museum of Can Tho is one that we will visit over our few days here too. Turning a corner and we are sad to see a guy on a motorbike selling puppies in a cage on the back, it cannot be pleasant for the animals in this heat – we just hope they go to good homes. We spend some time by the river, the obligatory statue of Ho Chi Minh takes pride of place, but it does offer some shade to the bench placed a few metres behind it.

I finally manage to purchase some flip-flops; they appear to be of decent quality but only time will tell. With our spending on clothing not complete we both buy hats from the local market before heading to a tourist office to enquire about a Mekong River excursion. We are shown various trips that they do and we opt for an individual tour, quite a bit more expensive but for what you get it seems reasonable, plus we had done the group tour on our previous visit that our memories are still scarred by! Alarm clocks will need to be set tomorrow; we have not done that for a long while...

To celebrate booking the excursion we head to the Mekong Inn and have a couple of beers. More teachers chatting away in the background – tough life they have! The menu looks good, quite a European offering and despite loving our meal last night it was a long way from our hotel, especially when we have spent most the day walking around.

By evening we wander around the food market again, rice pancakes will keep our hunger at bay for a little longer whilst we look around a clothes market. I try on some shorts but although my waist would fit, they are so tight around the legs, another pair fits but the button holes have been sewn, a definite design flaw! We conclude that clothes here are designed for locals, not the tourists - barely anything bigger than a thirty-two-inch waist...

Beefsteak is our choice from the Mekong Inn menu, hopefully a very safe option with being out on a boat for most of tomorrow morning. Although not a steak as we know it, we are not disappointed. It is obviously a popular place to eat here as there are no free tables by the time we have finished and people are being turned away.

An early night for us, the alarm is set for the middle of the night; well 4:45 a.m. - so as near as!

15th December

We are in reception for five o' clock, and they have kindly provided us with a breakfast carry out. Bread, cream cheese, bananas and cakes we are more than happy with that spread!

Our first thought is just how busy the streets are at this time of day; stall holders are already either set up or setting up, food is being cooked and people are out exercising. They have the right idea, it is still nice and cool at this time, by 9 a.m. it will be thirty-degree plus. We arrive at the tourist office in suitable time and are soon joined by our guides, it turns out that the young girl is learning the ropes and is here for the experience, so two guides for the price of one!

It is just a quick walk down to the riverside where we board our boat. There are a few other tourists about but we are outnumbered heavily by the locals going about their daily routines. Upon boarding we are each given a woven 'southern muffler' scarf as a gift, and with the temperature as it is we are happy to wear for now. Our guides are very chatty and informative, Cai Rang wholesale market will be our first port of call. It has a bustling atmosphere about the place, each boat will be selling just the one item and you know what that is as they hang it from the mast. Primarily it is a fruit market; melons, pineapples, onions, bananas and so on. The people buying must have their own fruit and veg stalls as they fill their boat up with a mix, popping from one seller to another until they have enough to return with for their customers.

Next stop is a rice noodle factory, no doubt a regular point on the tourist trail as other vendors are selling food snacks; iced coffees, potato cakes, the pancakes again... The noodle factory is interesting as we are taken through the various stages of production and can wander around and see them grinding, mixing and kneading, before eventually being rolled out onto boards and put in the sun to dry out before being cut into the noodle that we all recognise.

Another market, but this time more of a retail market that seems aimed at the tourist rather than the locals. Why would locals take a boat trip all this way when there are traders on dry land who have already collected fresh produce from the wholesaler at Cai Rang? It is good fun though, we are given pomelos and pineapple to try, both fresh and juicy. By now the heat is getting there so we remove our scarves and sit on them, these boats could do with more padding on the seats...

Leaving the mighty Mekong River, we branch off to the peace and quiet of the canals. The scenery is stunning as you pass through remote villages and view the countryside covered in rice fields, ducking under wooden bridges that give the locals access to each side. We stop and walk through an orchard before reaching a rice field, our hosts explain about what they are growing, the various stages and just general information about how the locals live. We manage to negotiate what they call a monkey bridge, we felt safe crossing but I was concerned about losing a flip-flop, I only bought them yesterday! Weaving our way through the backwaters that criss-cross the countryside we re-join the Mekong, and with that it is a case of working our way back to the pier where the day began in semi-darkness. We thank and tip our guides before looking for something to eat.

Right by our hotel is a lady who has a few plastic tables and a small menu, she is always busy with Vietnamese diners so that is a good sign. We must have arrived before the midday rush and there is a table free, two plates of pork, prawn, vegetables and noodles are served to us in no time. The lady then brings us over some chillies, she wasn't sure if we would like the added spice, but we love the heat. Another simple but delicious meal, and again we have both been fed for a paltry amount.

A siesta and a non-descript evening follow, what with such an early start and all that fresh air we are shattered, home and bed by ten!

16th December

We both slept like the proverbial log. It is a leisurely breakfast, there does seem to be a few more options than the other day, but we go for the peanut butter just the same. Today is our last full day in Can Tho before we fly on to Danang and make our way to Hoi An tomorrow.

Overcast skies greet us for what seems like the first time in ages, we are not complaining – in fact, it is a relief! The Museum of Can Tho is planned for today; we are just not sure how long that will keep us occupied for? The museum is free, so our expectations are immediately lowered! It is pleasant and cool inside, but apart from the part relating to the Mekong aspect there is not much that we haven't seen before. There is the usual mix of recovered artefacts and clothing through different eras, but not all of it is translated into English. We manage to make our visit last for ninety minutes, but in all honesty that was pushing it, fairly repetitive or perhaps we have just visited too many of these museums?

With nothing else planned we explore the nooks and crannies of the city and discover a further market and some interesting buildings. Whilst visiting a temple we get chatting to a friendly monk who gives us a bit of an insight on how he spends his day, from what we can make out from his broken English he is still training rather than a professional Monk (if there is such a thing?). By the riverside is the Ong Pagoda that we have walked by on numerous occasions, it has been the colours shining in the sun that have drawn our eyes to it, so for the first time we look inside. It is like many in HCMC, small but colourful, even the railings are painted in multiple bright shades, red, yellow, green... Reading about it further this is a Chinese Taoist Temple, and one of the oldest buildings in the city.

A spot of lunch from the Saigon Bakery before heading back to our room, bags to pack. Clean clothes put out for tomorrows travel, check flight times (for about the fourth time) and relax for a couple of hours playing travel scrabble.

It is our final evening here so we head back to the stainless-steel tables of the first place we ate, more pointing at pictures of food, another cheap bill and then head back to the Mekong Inn for a beer or two. The main street has been all lit up tonight, leaving us puzzled initially – there must be a festival of some kind going on? It takes a while before the penny drops; Christmas is less than ten days away.

Hoi An

17th December

The best breakfast yet, it must be the Hau Giang 2 hotels parting gift to us. Iced coffee, fruit, ham, cheese and pastries – a proper banquet. Before leaving we have some paperwork to sort out, luckily for us the reception staff here speak particularly good English and we can make them understand that we need to print a document, sign it, and then have it scanned and emailed back to us. We are very appreciative and ask if we need to pay for the service, but smiley reception lady says no, she is happy to help.

Hailing a taxi outside is no problem, again the language barrier crops up but sticking our arms out like an aeroplane and hand actions convey what we are after. He responds with his own plane impression and we say yes, yes with our thumbs up! Luggage boarded and we soon pick up signs for the airport, so thankfully we were all in harmony.

Our flight is delayed by twenty minutes, but other than that it is a smooth experience, the flight time is only a little over the hour so you are no sooner up in the air before the descent begins. Arrival at Danang takes us by surprise, a far bigger airport than what we thought it would be, but we soon find our driver who has been arranged by the Bamboo Garden Homestay. We are also surprised by the weather; it is not very nice and distinctively cool...

As we approach Hoi An we once again recognise bits from our previous stay. The part of town where our accommodation is situated is further along the river, a little beyond where we ventured last time. Our hosts at the Bamboo Garden are very friendly; entry is through a tailor's shop and our room is on the first floor. Anyone who has ever been Hoi An will know that it is famous for its tailors, there are hundreds of them across the town and many people travel there especially to get clothes made, the service and quality is considered that highly.

Our room is small but with lovely décor, dark woods and trim. Once again hot water, although it takes a little figuring out. We have use of a balcony but it is not attached to our room; to access it we must walk through another room and pass by their family spirit house. The view from the balcony is fantastic, it looks across the road and then there is the Thu Bon River just behind that. A spirit house is like a shrine to relatives who have passed, family members leave gifts there, sometimes fruit but more often cigarettes or sweets – whatever they enjoyed while they were alive.

For those not familiar with Hoi An it is a UNESCO World Heritage Site and a photographer's dream. Hoi An is known for being an exceptionally well-preserved South East Asian trading port. The history of its heyday between the fifteenth and nineteenth centuries is reflected in its architecture, a mix of eras and styles from wooden Chinese shophouses and temples to colourful French colonial buildings, Vietnamese tube houses and the iconic symbol of the town itself, the Japanese Covered Bridge with its pagoda. It is also this mix of influences from all over Asia that is responsible for the diversity in the local food dishes, supposedly making it the best in the whole of Vietnam.

The cool weather has deteriorated further since we arrived, as we head out for food there is drizzle in the air. With a ten-minutes' walk we are in Hoi An old town itself, so at least we are close to the restaurants. It is not the night for aimlessly wandering around so we head into the first one that looks busy, the Blue Dragon. The starter of 'wrap and roll' was very good but the mains did not reach such heights. On the plus side the local beer, Larue, was cheap.

Upon returning to our homestay, we are given a breakfast list, the options look very traditional so will need further research. We both order the local noodles, coffee and banana shakes, other items need further investigation, time is on our side – lots of breakfasts here ahead of us.

18th December

We had slept well until a nearby rooster went mad! We managed to sleep for a little longer before heading downstairs for breakfast. We are led out into a garden where breakfast will be served under a pergola. Another couple from London join us, they have cookery lessons planned for today – something we may consider if the weather forces us indoors. The coffee is superb, and the local noodles are top of the noodles chart, thicker than most we have tried. If that's how good breakfast is here, roll on tomorrow morning.

Before heading out we drop our laundry off at reception, our host tries upselling us some new shirts, trousers, skirts... We explain that we have no way of carrying any more luggage, as lovely as her work is. The weather is still on the drizzly side, not really what we had been expecting. A bit of research shows that although the average temperature for December is high it does fluctuate a lot; maybe we have made an error, or are we just a little unlucky? Time will tell.

The damp conditions do not put us off as we head into town, we wander around looking at menus (always thinking of food), check out a few cooking classes, bike tours, coracle experiences... we just need the weather to take a turn for the better. We buy donuts, not because were hungry but we just like donuts. We also buy some coffee making equipment, there is a kettle in the room but that is all – now we will be able to sit on that balcony and enjoy an early-morning coffee.

Back at the homestay we put the kettle on and have a trial run, perfect. Eventually the weather improves so we walk back into town and explore the other side of the bridge, this is where the night market that we have read about takes place. We also discover the Red Gecko restaurant that our hosts have recommended to us. We pop inside for a drink and get chatting to a pair of older guys from New Zealand, they are living the high life and are looking good on it. They undoubtedly have a bigger budget than us, their talking about business class flights and hotels with butlers – we never found any of them when we were selecting rooms at ten pound per night or under!

We return to the Red Gecko later in the day for our evening meal; as well as tailors Hoi An is also famous for its quality of food, so we have lofty expectations. The spring rolls to start are stunning, flaky but not greasy and just delicious - we should have ordered a plate each rather than sharing! The mains of crispy wontons and the cao lau, a dish regional to Hoi An, matched the standard of the starter, perhaps our best meal yet?

19th December

Yesterday's drizzle has turned to rain, the weather is getting worse! On the plus side the rooster never woke us this morning and the coffee is to die for. Breakfast wise, Alison tries the sticky rice and peanuts but finds it a bit stodgy for her liking while I have the local rice cakes, which I find delicious despite a weird texture. Mango and pineapple juices are our fruity shakes of the day.

We enquire about a trip to Hue, more because of the frustration with the weather than anything else. We consider our options but with our next flight leaving from Danang it would then mean back-tracking on ourselves, plus we have already paid for our accommodation here so the extra travelling and other costs involved put us off the idea.

As if to cheer us up the weather improves, blue skies but the ominous rain clouds are never far away – it is toying with us, daring us to go out on the free bikes that the homestay provides. With the theory that any rain will be warm rain we take the chance, albeit with raincoats in the front basket. We cycle around the surrounding countryside for a good few hours, the roads are good with not much traffic and it is all very flat which makes it easy going. There is some lovely scenery as you leave the town, paddy fields with raised banks criss-crossing fields, coconut groves and the odd buffalo wandering around... Our raincoats are on and off a handful of times, but nothing drastic. On a couple of occasions we cross paths with another cycling group, we wonder if they have more idea of where they are or where their heading than us? At one point we find the beach, which is handy as the first sunny day and that will be our destination.

By mid-afternoon we have found our way back into Hoi An, we were never technically lost, we just were not sure where we were at times! The elderly guys from New Zealand are here again, lunchtime cocktails for them, our budget stretches to a beer each. All this exercise has left us hungry, so we head off in search of the Phi Banh Mi food stall. Banh Mi is a Vietnamese roll, think small French stick, stuffed with pork, pate, pickled vegetables and mayonnaise or chilli jam depending on how spicy you like your food. Phi Banh Mi is the number one restaurant in the town on Tripadvisor – and this is the only thing on his menu. We opt for the Vietnamese special, served warm the bread is soft and crusty but the fillings are something else, smooth pate with the crunch of the vegetables, pork just falling apart – I am beginning to drool just writing about it...

On our way back to base we book cooking lessons at the Om restaurant for tomorrow morning, we also buy some brandy and coke for a nightcap later this evening.

Rather than a restaurant meal this evening we go alfresco at Mr Hi's food stall on the other side of the river. Again, the food is excellent; wontons, fried noodles and special noodles with 'fresh' beer. Very friendly owners, obviously very much a family business as its Mrs Hi doing all the waiting on customers. The bench tables mean you just sit wherever you can and chat to your fellow diners. No sooner have we finished our meal and it starts raining, properly this time, so we are quite soggy by the time we arrive back at the Bamboo Gardens.

20th December

Another contender for best breakfast so far! It seems rather naughty to order banana pancakes for breakfast, even more so when they are drizzled with condensed milk... The fruit salad was excellent too, its biggest flaw being that it was not a pancake.

This morning is our cookery class at the Om Restaurant; before we don our aprons, we are taken around the market to buy ingredients for the dishes that we will be cooking. As well as cooking it is also a learning experience as there are so many fruits and vegetables that we do not recognise, lots of stuff at this market is not on the shelves at Tesco's!

Back in the restaurant and we get introduced to the chef, our teacher for the morning – let the cooking commence. With chopping blocks and knives at the ready we set about the shredding and dicing of the veg, then cut the pork into thin slivers, peel the shrimps, blend the spices, and then prepare a dipping sauce! With a hot pan we have soon created the filling for our starter; fresh spring rolls. It would be nice to say the rolls were rolled as neatly and tightly as the chefs, but hey, he has had far more practise than us. Either way it should not affect the taste.

For the main course we create a sauteed beef with cashew nuts, marinating the beef in a blend of spices while we do the rest of the prepping. More chopping and dicing before adding more seasoning. Lots of spring onions in this one, it must be healthy! Cooking again is very quick on a high heat and once plated up ours looks just as good as chefs!

To accompany the main course we knock up a mango and shrimp salad, no flames involved this time as the shrimps were taken aside and cooked by chef whilst we were making the spring rolls. We love the salads over here and this is a great insight to why they are just crammed with flavour. There is no salad cream over here, instead they use mint leaves, garlic, chilli sauce, lime juice and fish sauces to create a taste that just makes a plain salad taste divine. Using a rolling pin, we then bash up a few peanuts into a dust to sprinkle on top, it creates another texture and taste – genius!

Having done all this arduous work, we now must eat it, we are led to the best seats in the restaurant, a balcony looking out over the Thu Bon River – we can watch the circular splashes from the rain whilst we eat! Bursting at the seams already and they compound our suffering when they bring out flambeed bananas as a desert, liberally coated in a chocolate sauce; we are now at the stage when moving is almost impossible... As we leave, we are given gifts as a reminder of our cooking class, vegetable peelers – identical to the ones we bought on our last visit.

The rain looks set in for today so we head back to the Bamboo Garden for a lazy afternoon. A couple of coffees on the balcony and a few more games of scrabble in our World Series.

By evening the rain has abated, we venture into Hoi An and cross the river for the night market. It really is beautiful as the lanterns are all lit up and people are buying candles to float down the river. The market is busy, everyone is out tonight having spent the day cooped up avoiding the rain. Still stuffed from our three-course dinner we just graze at food stalls tonight rather than sitting down for a meal.

21st December

The weather is now becoming annoying, grey and overcast again. Breakfast provides us with temporary cheer, once again we go for the pancakes.

Alisons birthday is Christmas Eve and we plan to treat ourselves both on that night and the following - Christmas Day! We spend the morning browsing Tripadvisor for recommendations, Christmas Day we ideally want to re-visit a restaurant called Son which is out of Hoi An itself, on the road to Cao Dai beach. Of everywhere we ate when in Vietnam in April this place really stood out; the setting, the friendly owner, and the food. A visit to an Indian restaurant for Alisons birthday would be good, there's a couple that have excellent reviews so we will have a walk by each of them, see if a particular menu swings it one way or another.

On our way out the daughter of the family (who speaks the most / best English) tries to sell us a Christmas Gala Dinner at the nearby Lanterns Hotel – it looks very pricey when you are on our budget! We tell her we have already made plans, which is nearly true.

Walking into Hoi An we pause by the Lantern Hotel, yes it does look grand, but in all honesty, we have no clothes with us suitable for a posh gala meal. Heading out of Hoi An we look in the windows of the first Indian restaurant that we are considering, it looks a standard menu and reasonable prices. The road towards Cao Dai seems to go on and on, we know the Son restaurant is on this road as we biked past it the other day! Eventually we get there and book a table, we hope it is still under the same ownership as before, we don't recognise the young lady who takes our booking.

The trek back into Hoi An seems to take an age, we should have borrowed the bikes from the homestay. On the plus side it has stayed fine, and the weather seems to be warming up – maybe things are changing? Once in town we find the Ganesh restaurant, slightly more expensive but looks a lot nicer and the location is also a lot better for us, so we book that one for the twenty-fourth.

As we wander further away from the river, we find a hostel selling the legendary fresh beer or 'Bia Hoi'. Often billed as the worlds cheapest beer it contains no preservatives and is only between three and four percent alcohol content. It is because there are no preservatives it takes the name fresh beer due to its limited lifespan. The price here is three thousand Vietnamese dong; and were getting just over thirty-three thousand dong to our pound, on the downside that is a price per half rather than a pint! It would be rude not to try a couple, which then turns into three, four – yes, it is very drinkable.

With a beer induced hunger we visit Phi Banh Mi; he is doing a roaring trade and we have to wait patiently for a table, his fame means that he is now a stop-off point for some walking tours as it is a huge group that get up and leave at the same time. The short wait was well worthwhile.

It sounds like we are always eating, our late afternoon was spent on the balcony reading and watching the world go by. Showered and changed we are back in town and again visit Mr Hi at his food stall on the far side of the river, more local dishes – white rose, wontons and the cao lau and noodles again. Our 'neighbours' are eating a rolled-up pancake dish which we haven't tried, must remember to try that one.

22nd December

Breakfast of pho bo (beef noodles) and bun xaou (a beef noodle salad) are a change from the pancakes. We do get a sweet fix from the passion fruit juice and an iced coffee. Say it quietly but the weather is looking better today, no sun splitting the pavements but it is definitely trying....

With optimism high we wander into town for some more coffee and to pick up another bottle of coke, with the weather continuing to improve we head back to base to pack our beach bag and borrow their bikes.

It is about a twenty-five-minute bike ride to Cao Dai beach; the sea is rough and there is not much beach either! Nothing can put us off though, the sun is out and we are going to make the most of it. We sit and read for a few hours, but also get chatting to someone who recommends An Bang beach, just a further ten minutes up the coast, if the weather has taken a turn for the better we will visit there tomorrow. Having finally got sand on our flip-flops we bike back to Hoi An, stopping for an ice cream on the way.

Our evening meal is again spent at Mr Hi's, the rolled-up pancakes that we had enviously looked on last night were truly tasty, we think we have now tried every dish on his menu! We enjoy a couple of beers on the way home in a bar immediately opposite to the ferry that travels between Hoi An and the little habited island of Cam Kim. No sooner has the ferry boarded all the scooters and its off again. Cam Kim is a tiny island situated within the river Thu Bon, rather than the more familiar idea of an island off the coast.

To round off what has been a good day we buy a small bottle of brandy and have a nightcap sat on the balcony...

23rd December

Disaster; the wrong breakfast, we both ordered the fried rice but instead got the sticky rice which we are not so keen on. The weather is overcast but definite signs for optimism, so being very much the glass half full type, we borrow the bikes – destination An Bang beach.

We find our way, slightly off course at one point, but a local put us back on the right track with a bit of pointing and gesturing. It all looks more promising even before we see the beach, various stalls are providing bicycle lock up services, the first guy wants to charge us forty thousand dong, that seems overpriced to us so we move onto the next. Purely by chance, or by not taking the first option, we discover a stall selling water for ten thousand which includes free bicycle parking, a great result!

By now the sun has beaten back the cloud and the day just keeps getting better, the beach is good, soft golden sand, a gentle slope down to the sea and sunbeds for hire. The sunbed seller explains that they are free if you spend so much on food; he has a small menu with assorted options, or thirty thousand dong if you choose not to eat – that seems fair enough. The beach is busy but not packed, and after reading for a little while we decide it is time to venture into the sea. The water is very warm but a bit choppy and the undulating sand makes it difficult to negotiate, Alison, much to my amusement, loses balance and resurfaces spluttering and pulling her bikini bottoms back up!

We manage almost five hours in all, which for us is a long, long time! The combination of comfortable sunbeds, an enjoyable book and plenty to see has made that time fly by. Fishing boats pass on a regular basis and watching how they manoeuvre the coracles with a stirring motion has me in awe, surely something that is round has no back or front – they defy boating logic. We settle our bill, not having eaten we pay the price for the bed hire and head back to our bikes.

We find our way back to Hoi An without getting lost, and pop for a quick banh mi and then a beer at the bar opposite the ferry. For some reason, and we will never know why there is a big white chicken wandering around wearing a large black crucifix, think James Brown in the Blues Brothers film. We had seen the same chicken last night, but with it being dark had not been able to work out what was around its neck.

After showering, resting, coffee and reading we head back out, dropping off our laundry at reception as we leave. On the way into town we spot some attractive Christmas decorations, they might be nice to take home to add to our collection. We try a different restaurant this evening, For You; not our greatest decision, the duck and pork dishes were both just ok while the rice pancakes were very greasy. We should have stuck with Mr Hi.

Christmas Eve

Alisons birthday! With it being a special occasion banana pancakes oozing with condensed milk did not feel so indulgent, even when they are for breakfast.

Today the sun is properly out, none of this peeking through the clouds nonsense. What better way to spend a birthday than on the beach, sun sea and sand? The beach is a lot busier than yesterday; we had noticed that our homestay was too, there was a good few having breakfast this morning and it looked like all the garden lodges were occupied too.

Not a lot to tell, the day panned out just like the previous one, people watching, paddling, reading and just chilling out. On our way back we spoil ourselves, an ice-cream on route home before stopping for the now regular banh mi. We also need to withdraw some more money, and it just so happens that the MB Bank is right by the Bia Hoi place...

Back in the room and connected to Wi-Fi all the birthday greetings start to come flooding through! The UK being seven hours behind Vietnam means that friends and family at home are only just getting up. We speak to Lauren, and are pleased to hear that all is well with everyone back home. It is curry night for us tonight, a proper treat, and fortunately our laundry has been done, and is neatly folded. Wearing our finest clothes, and not looking too crumpled we head out to Ganesh for tea.

The restaurant is heaving as we arrive, so it was lucky that we had made a reservation. The staff are very welcoming and friendly as they lead us to our table, the food that we can see looks incredibly good and there looks to be plenty of it. We opt for our usual Indian routine; poppadoms, two mains, one side, one rice and one naan, then share the lot! As Indian meals go it was top notch, the spice level and heat of the Madras and Jalfrezi comparable to what we get back at home. The presentation was different however, rather than standard crockery it was eaten off gold metal plates. Our drinks were served in gold tankards too, all in all it was a great evening – and for the first time in ages, not a chopstick in sight!

A couple of Gin and Tonics on the way home to round off the Birthday celebrations.

Christmas Day

Christmas day! A first, neither of us have ever started Christmas morning with a breakfast of fried rice. To be honest it just feels like any other day over here, only the sun looks like it is not coming out to play.

Wandering into town and it is just a normal day, the veg market is in full flow, the ferry is loading up and all the locals are out just doing their 'normal' every day thing. We check out the jewellers by one of the bridges, Alison likes a necklace they have, a thin silver chain with a Vietnamese hat on it. Never ones to spend at the first place (remember the bike storage), we browse in other places too. Across the other side of the river we sit and enjoy a few beers, and in a nod to what day it is we line up our empties in the shape of a Christmas tree!

Heading back home we re-visit the jewellers and venture inside, negotiating a price for that necklace but also with one eye on a Pandora charm, a return visit may well be on the cards.

Once back at the homestay we can make WhatsApp calls back home and Alison speaks to both of her sisters. With it being Christmas rather than enjoying afternoon coffees on the balcony we switch to brandy. Alison calls home again as her Mum and Dad should be at her sisters by now, so is able to chat with them for the first time in two months.

Tonight we are on the road out towards Cao Dai, and our reservation at the Son restaurant. Misjudging exactly how far it was when we went to book, we choose to borrow the bikes for tonights visit. The owner remembers us from the last visit and we are equally pleased to see him and that it has not changed hands! From the specials board we choose the belly pork for one dish and the pork and squid in a tamarind sauce for the second. The belly pork is served with two types of leaves, one large and green the other soft like velvet but pink (no idea what they are). You use these leaves to roll around the belly pork and then dip into the sauce, to this day one of the best meals we have ever eaten.

The owner kindly gives us a free dessert and some tea before we settle the bill and say our goodbyes. Maybe we can fit one more visit in before we leave...

Back at the room we ring Lauren, knowing that she will be at my Mum and Dads for Christmas day, my Mum seems very giggly, cannot even blame the Christmas sherry as she does not drink! Any way all is well there too, they have just finished dinner as we prepare to sit on the balcony with a nightcap.

Boxing Day

Once again, the weather is cloudy. Equally uninspiring was our breakfast choice, why did we choose omelettes?

After a lazy morning of surfing on our phones we wander into town, trailing the same streets so often has made us more than ready to move on. With there only being two more days before our flight to Hanoi, please can tomorrow be sunny for one last beach day? We are pleased to see who we christened 'religious chicken' again, for two days there had been no sign of him, we thought he had gone to meet his maker. With the weather drizzly again we stop and have a coffee, watch the world go by. We have a second and watch a bit more – it is one of those kinds of days.

Food at Mr Hi's, a beer in a bar showing the football on the way back home. There is nothing like being in a Vietnamese bar, sat next to an Australian and both being delighted that Manchester United are losing! Another beer before heading back home for the night, fingers crossed for the weather tomorrow...

27th December

It is our last full day in Hoi An. Very traditional in our breakfast choices this morning, banh beo and Vietnams most famous dish, pho. It does seem that the country loves pho that much it can be ate as a meal any time of day. Could we adopt that idea with fish and chips...?

Crossing our fingers worked, the sun is shining right from the off, so we cycle down to the beach. We only spend a couple of hours there; we are both out of reading material so apart from people watching not much else to do. How do these professional sun bathers manage day after day, hour after hour without ever getting bored, or uncomfortable? The sea is rougher today so a paddle to cool off is as much as we manage.

We enjoy the bike ride back, taking a different route via Cao Dai and then following that road into town. It will be good to move on, as much as we have enjoyed Hoi An we seem to have pounded the same streets, beautiful as they are for long enough. The afternoon is a lazy affair, coffee on the balcony, sorting out our bags, another coffee...

We have one final walk into Hoi An, earlier than our normal evening visit, Alison wants to visit the jewellers again. It is still open and a Vietnamese hat 'Pandora style' is bought to compliment the necklace. Walking by the Blue Dragon one of the prime tables is free on their veranda, so we have a beer as the sun sets before heading across the bridge to Mr Hi's for our last meal there – excellent as usual. We finish off the evening on the balcony at the Bamboo Gardens with a brandy each.

Hanoi

28th December

We have been away for two months today, in some ways it seems an age, but in others time has flown by. We are first up this morning for breakfast, with a flight to catch we had set an alarm but more out of paranoia than believing we would oversleep.

Our homestay family give us an enthusiastic send off as we are collected from the front gates, and our driver has us at Danang airport within the half hour – as usual we are incredibly early for our check in! The boards have our flight as departing on time so we bring out the travel Scrabble to kill the time.

Landing in Hanoi after a particularly good flight, our first with Vietnam Airways – our initial thought is how cool the temperature is. Fortunately, we are not hanging about for too long as we soon spot the driver holding a board with our names that the Indochina Queen 2 has sent to collect us. The driver speaks minimal English so the journey is made in near silence. Looking out the windows of the car we hope to see some landmarks that we recognise, but on this occasion not a thing. When we do arrive at our hotel it is on a bustling street, scooters parked everywhere and a cacophony of noise – right in the heart of the Old Quarter.

Our room is not ready when we first arrive, so we leave our bags with reception and go for a walk. Once we are nearer to the Hoan Kiem lake we soon have our bearings; we are close to the hotel we stayed at in April. We stop at the Lotteria (like a Vietnamese version of McDonalds), and have a burger and fries; the last time we arrived in Hanoi it was the evening of the fortieth anniversary of the Vietnam War ending, and the Lotteria was the only place we could get food from. The whole city was heaving and restaurants were all fully booked, fast food was the only option! On the plus side the anniversary celebrations gave us the best firework display that we have ever seen.

Back at the hotel and we are shown to our room, except it was more of a cupboard. We look at our booking on Hotels.com; we have booked into a deluxe double room, the pictures of the room look spacious, nothing like what we have been given. Rather than unpack we take it up with reception and after a little negotiation, and a small additional charge, we reach a compromise. One to take up with Hotels.com at a future date! Our new room has views across the street, a big thirty-two-inch television and a whole lot more space, and once again hot water.

Because we visited Halong Bay on our last visit we are looking to head off into the Sapa Mountains for a few days this time. The hotel offers that excursion and the price looks in line with what we had seen this afternoon in various tour agencies, we get more information and make a booking.

Tonight is the first time that we have needed the fleeces that we travelled out in; it is not raining but there is a dampness in the air. We make our way to the lake before walking all the way around it, there are illuminations all the way and Happy New Year signs in both English and Vietnamese. They are also in the process of putting up some scaffolding and a stage in readiness for the celebrations, not sure they would meet with our health and safety standards as parts are perched on wood where it overhangs the kerb...

For our food we eat at the New Day restaurant, on a three-course set menu. Tables are positioned outside on the street but they do have proper adult sized chairs... Fried spring rolls starter, a sauteed beef and vegetables dish with steamed rice for the main and a dessert of custard, the food was good but the service was awfully slow. Just around the corner we discover a Bia Hoi so sit on a street corner watching the mayhem from a plastic stool, you cannot have a night out in Vietnam without sitting on a plastic stool!

29th December

We slept ok last night, but being to the front of the building it does get quite noisy as the shops begin to open. It does not help that we are on 'kitchenware' street, where every shop sells metal utensils, pans etc. With hindsight we should have booked a hotel on 'cotton' street.

If we were woken up earlier than we would have liked the buffet breakfast more than makes amend. There is a diverse spread, both of local food but also of hams and cheese, fruit, cakes and yoghurts. The coffee is not hot enough though.

First an explanation about the streets selling just one range of items. Hanoi's Old Quarter is made up of thirty-six streets, each street name starts Hang which means a series of stores. These names go back hundreds of years, so some no longer sell what the name implies, such as Hang Thung (barrels) and Hang Lo Ren (blacksmiths). Others still trade in the same items all these years later; Hang Bac (jewellers), Hang Da (leather) and Hang Hai Tuong (shoes). The theory behind this is that everyone knows exactly what street they want to be at for the best selection of that item. The one that you wouldn't have wanted to be needing to visit was Hang Lo Sú, shop after shop selling coffins...

Rain is steadily pouring this morning so we head off with an umbrella in hand. First stop is St Joseph's where there is a wedding in progress, we are beckoned inside so get to see the interior as well as the outside of this impressive building. Still trying to shelter from the rain we visit a high-end shopping mall, very posh inside, luxury brands galore – interestingly far more staff than customers. We walk a little further, make a withdrawal from the bank and instantly become dong millionaires before heading back to the Indochina Queen to pay for our Sapa excursion.

We relax in the room for a while, waiting and hoping for the weather to improve, luckily for us it does – so back out again. We visit a typical Hanoi 'Tube House', this one is a heritage site but you immediately get the feel of what they must be like to live in, and that is dark. They are called tube houses due to their very narrow frontage, yet once you are inside they go back, and back, and back. Many would even have a courtyard in between the front rooms and the buildings at the rear, this would then allow light into the rooms. In some ways they are not dissimilar to a mid-terrace house in the UK, only much, much narrower.

Walking around the lake we visit the Opera House at the southern tip, and although an old building it is nowhere near as impressive as the one in HCMC. We browse in a few shops, the usual tat to take home, fridge magnets, T- Shirts, mugs etc.

For our evening meal we visit a restaurant called Gecko. There are a few of them scattered around the city, they all have different offers and the foods Western; it is good to have a night off noodles and rice – and the twelve-inch sub is really tasty. They have burger and pizza options so might visit again, with the weather being cool in the evenings it is also good to be inside eating and with proper tables and chairs.

30th December

Look out of the window and it is raining again. Breakfast adds to our disappointment, not a patch on yesterday's offering. The hot food was cold and there was no cereal or cake, it is not a good start to the day!

One good thing about being in Hanoi is that there are plenty of museums to wander around on rainy days. Even museums that would not initially float your boat are so cheap to enter that they are worth the gamble. By 10 a.m. we have made our way to the south of the lake and are in the Vietnamese Women's Museum, a large five-storey building that has three permanent exhibitions exploring women's role in family, history and fashion.

Must say that we found it better than we had anticipated, in fact it was very good! Exploring the family section was a revelation, it took you all the way through the course of their lives, education, marriage, becoming mothers and the role they have within the family. Some of the jobs that are male dominated in Europe and beyond are the job of the lady of the house in Vietnam, cultivation and fishing stood out. They are also burdened with the more traditional roles, cooking and dress making, but not just for the family household, so many have their own businesses and make a good living. The Vietnamese woman really is the head of the house.

The history side, as in every museum we have visited in Vietnam does, focuses on the Vietnam, or American War, as they always refer to it. If we hadn't just seen the first exhibition, we might have believed that women in Vietnam did not exist until the 1950s. One thing we did learn is that they are not to be messed with, their wartime contribution was far more than we ever realised, something that tends to be glossed over when film makers give their version of history.

Fashion, well Alison enjoyed this section far more than me! It was costumes through the ages, and how fashion has changed – it got less frilly is my uneducated verdict. Of more interest was the distinct traditions and outfits of the ethnic communities; we were surprised that there are fifty-four officially recognised, and they are predominantly based in the north of the country - a taster of what we will see in the Sapa Mountains.

We thought we had finished, but the best, or most relatable part was still to come. The street vendors! Wandering around Hanoi you are never far away from ladies pushing bicycles or carts around laden with flowers, or carrying fruit and vegetables on a pole with a basket at each end filled with the produce - be that in the heat of the day (not in December!) or late into the evening. Trying out the carrying pole for ourselves, we are shocked at just how heavy it is, that is one tough job! It does explain why you see so many wandering around selling donuts, that is a far lighter and wiser option. The benefit of the pole is that you can get down the narrow lanes that the carts are too big for, which means you can get to the prime selling slots first; fortune favours the hardiest of ladies in Vietnam.

Upon leaving the museum the weather has taken a turn for the better, no sun but it is at least fine. We explore the streets around the west of the lake and discover the food street that we have read about, it is a small area but with a big choice of food options – a visit to this part of the city one evening beckons? We mooch around a bit more before we sit down and have a bad coffee; most unusual, the taste is normally strong but this was more like a nasty powdered supermarket own brand. Luckily, we find a Bia Hoi just around the corner so stop again, anything to wash away the taste of that coffee...

After a disappointing breakfast and coffee, we round off the day with a disappointing evening meal, they say things come in threes. The Countryside Restaurant, great reviews on Tripadvisor, lovely seats on a veranda overlooking the streets but very average food, the highlight was seeing two guys on a scooter transporting a double mattress from our elevated vantage point!

New Year's Eve

It seems breakfast here is a lottery; we are up slightly earlier, perhaps that's the secret. A full selection, its hot and a couple of cups of coffee have set us up perfectly for another long walk. Today we are going to see Uncle Ho at the Ho Chi Minh mausoleum before heading further north to the Ho Tay Lake, and fortunately the weather is fine.

It is a proper trek to the mausoleum, starting off in the tight streets of the Old Quarter before they open out onto grand boulevards, government buildings and more foreign embassies occupy the properties around here. Once we are through here it opens out completely, we pass the Imperial Citadel with its great walls and tower before reaching the vast open spaces of Ba Dinh Square.

The Ho Chi Minh mausoleum is the centre piece, on a stepped raised platform the huge granite structure with its pillars tower above the soldiers in their all-white ceremonial uniforms. In the centre hall of this structure, behind transparent glass and dimmed lighting is where the embalmed body of Ho Chi Minh lies. The long banner to the left says 'Nước Cộng Hòa Xã Hội Chủ Nghĩa Việt Nam Muôn Năm' which translates as Long Live the Socialist Republic of Vietnam.

We walk around the outside of Ba Dinh Square to the entrance gate for visitors, the queue is not too long but suddenly we feel very under-dressed. The Vietnamese people have obviously got their best clothes on to pay their respects to 'Uncle Ho', we are wearing the best of what is clean. Once through the gates we follow the path to the mausoleum itself, as the queue gets nearer a noticeable hush falls upon the procession of visitors. By the time we reach the grand doors a silence has descended, in single file we slowly make our way around the central hall where his resting body is on display. It was a bizarre experience, considering that he passed in 1969 his body is extremely well preserved; not only is the mausoleum inspired by Lenin's in Moscow, it is also Russian scientists and experts that help keep his body in such good condition. To this day 'Uncle Ho' is allegedly sent back to Russia each year for a month or two makeover to preserve his body and maintain his facial features.

Whilst in the gardens behind we saw the one pillar pagoda, that dates right back to the eleventh century. The fact that it has been restored multiple times, as well as been relocated diminished the story for us! Nevertheless, it is an attractive building in its own right, but the reality is that it was built as recently as 1955, yet somehow it is regarded as one of Vietnams two most important temples; the other being the Perfume Temple in Hue.

We continue our walk to Lake Ho Tay, it is vast, far bigger than we imagined! Luckily for us the Tran Quoc Pagoda that we have seen in guidebooks is only a short distance away, set on what was once a small island that is accessible these days by a stone walkway. Founded in the sixth century this is the oldest pagoda in the city, a Buddhist site that unusually also worships female Buddhas, known as 'the Mothers'. The green Mother represents the mountains and forests, white Mother has domain over the water and the red Mother over the sky. It is a pilgrimage site in the first month of the lunar calendar, but also renowned for its sunset views...

It is a long walk back to the Indochina Queen, our legs and feet are aching by the time we get back, but with an early tea planned due to it being New Year's Eve we cannot rest up for long. Pizza and garlic bread at the Gecko before buying a small bottle of vodka and some coke ready for tonights celebrations, getting in anywhere for a drink will be impossible.

At 10 p.m. we make the short walk to the lake where the DJ is on the stage creating a party atmosphere. Lots of young people are about and our meagre drink selection is put to shame, they have gone down the full-on party route, crates of beer, bottles of spirits, more beer... The wait takes an age, no music that we recognise, but the locals are loving every minute; a countdown for the clock striking midnight and then a rather limp firework display. All that is left is to work our way through the crowds and back to the hotel.

New Year's Day

As we get up Happy New Year messages begin to ping through on our phones, we are all done with that and had sent ours out last night while friends and family were eating their teas. The breakfast selection is good again today.

Wandering around the market we still find it odd to see fruit and vegetables displayed alongside live turtles, fish and chickens. There is something that attracts us to these places, so vibrant and noisy but always smelly – and rarely in a pleasant way either. With the weather turning darker we head back to the room; we can prepare our bags ready for Sapa.

Squeezing our clothes into a sports bag is a tight fit, but at least this way we can leave the bulk of our luggage in storage. We settle our bill with reception and collect a printed itinerary for this trip. The Sapa Eden Hotel will be our accommodation and it looks excellent, and has really good reviews. This is going to be quite an upgrade to what we have become accustomed to. Flicking through the TV channels and Grease is on, obviously shown over the festive period here too – is it compulsory all around the world? We have missed the start but watch it anyway.

By now the rain has abated, we find a food stall that serves noodles, so opt for fast food tonight rather than a sit-down meal. Having eaten we find Ta Hien Street and more Bia Hoi, the party atmosphere from last night is still ongoing! It seems like a local band has set up in the street and is holding an open mic night, various people having a sing and some are obviously talented. On our way home we stumble across a group of waitresses who are turning the street into their own dancefloor, not sure what that is all about but not something you see every day!

Sapa Mountains

2nd January

It is an early morning alarm that wakes us from our slumber, first dibs at the buffet breakfast though. A driver picks us up and transfers us to the bus that will take us onto Sapa.

A very enjoyable bus journey, despite it being so long - there was a non-descript part from leaving the outskirts of Hanoi to reaching the mountains, but once we were onto the windy roads the views were stunning. The last hour of the drive was slow progress as we snaked our way up mountain sides, even passing through clouds at one point, not a journey for anyone who suffers from travel sickness. On arrival at the bus station we are collected by a private car and transferred to the Sapa Eden Hotel, the views across the valley below would have been even better if it were not for the damp mist!

Our room is unavailable but our lunch is ready, and it is a good spread of pork, fish, vegetables and rice. Rather than hang about reception until our room is ready, we head out to explore Sapa itself. Our first impressions are that it is more in keeping with a Swiss alpine resort, all very pretty and compact. We venture down one street and bars and restaurants are advertising their open fires, obviously it can turn very cold here at times.

By five thirty we are back at the hotel and shown to our room, it is clean and spacious and has amazing views from the balcony; the vista is that good that we keep our coats on and sit outside for a coffee. The bathroom is luxury, hot water and toiletries. Proper toiletries, not just a tiny bar of soap and toothbrush! Showered and changed we head out wearing our 'North Face' waterproofs that we purchased in Hanoi.

No sooner are we in the town and the lights all go out, one by one generators kick in at hotels and shops before full power is eventually restored; it did not seem to faze anyone so we suspect it is a regular occurrence. We browse menus before going for a set meal option and a bottle of wine, our first in over two months (must be a record for us). The soup starter was rich and creamy, spring rolls, vegetable curry and lemongrass chicken follow, a banana and honey pancake to finish, absolutely stuffed! We waddle back home, so much food we have demolished today, hiking around tomorrow will burn off some of those excess calories...

3rd January

For the second morning running we are woken by the alarm; it was a great sleep in a snug bed. We eat breakfast although we are not really that hungry, bread and omelette so nothing to write home about. Back to the room and we put on our walking gear, well in our case that is just our warmest clothes, the ones we left England in. We walk down to reception for eight o' clock, as per our itinerary, only to be told that it is another hour until our pick up. We could have spent a little longer in bed!

By the time the clock approaches 9 a.m. there are eight of us waiting in reception for the guides. The other six are all booked in to spend the night at a homestay and an onward hike tomorrow – it does explain the size of the bags that they have with them! Our walk-mates are a family of Australians, Mum, Dad and two teenagers and a young couple, he is also Australian while she is from Poland, but currently living in London. We all say our hellos and none of us are exactly sure what to expect, but this route is classed as light trekking.

We are collected from reception by a Hmong lady, one of the Indigenous groups that have made their home in the north of Vietnam. By the time we reach the bottom of the hotel drive there are a handful of others who smile, and nod but, do not speak. All starts off quite easy, light, as they call it – it is a gentle incline but still on the tarmacked road before suddenly we branch off down a more rural track. The going is gradually getting tougher, the rural track becomes a muddy trail and we are now working our way down the mountainside, into the valley below.

If you are familiar with images of the Sapa Mountains then you will know that their mountain sides are not like ours at home, they are made up of terraces, so like steps; unfortunately for us these steps are huge, about a three-foot drop from one terrace to the next. At times bumping your way down on your bottom is the adopted technique. With conditions damp and slippery it is not long before each one of our group has a muddy backside from where they have ended up on the floor. How these Hmong ladies keep their balance is a mystery!

On occasions the route looks impassable (as well as impossible), Alison has a Hmong lady keeping a very tight grip of her which she is grateful for, I am slip-sliding away close behind, enjoying it in a strange kind of way. Sometimes it is a case of grabbing hold of bushes to keep upright, but even that has a downside, some of them are prickly! Despite our difficulties the views are well worth it, the clouds come and go but when it is clear we can see the stream meandering and shimmering along the base of the valley, terrace after terrace on the mountains opposite and the odd ramshackle building scattered around.

Having navigated the terracing all the way down to the valley bottom, the walking again gets easier, we are back on a road of sorts. Our end point is in the distance and it is at this point that our Hmong guides turn into ruthless saleswomen! It is exceedingly difficult to say no, but we do get away with just a pair of woven bangles. It turns out that one of those ramshackle buildings that we had seen earlier was where our lunch is being served.

We sit with the young couple and have a good chat with them, she is working in film production and he works in IT for a finance company. We can give them a few recommendations as they are travelling Vietnam north to south, with both Hoi An and the Mekong delta to look forward to. Lunch is an ok affair; rice, noodles – we expected no other! As the meal finishes our fellow walkers are rounded up for a further short hike to the Homestay where they will be spending the night, before continuing their journey tomorrow.

A Hmong lady called Mo walks us onto the next village, around a mile or so away, where we will be picked up and returned into town. As our days hiking finishes the sun decides to make its first appearance of the day, how we could have done with that earlier!

Back in town we find a bar with magnificent views over Sapa, it has been a very enjoyable day, easy to say that now with a beer in hand. Alison has impressed herself, surprised at what she could physically do, but also not knowing whether to laugh or cry at certain points of the day... We pick up a bottle of wine for our room tonight, we won't be venturing far.

For the first time in our two months plus away the hot shower has never been so wanted or needed, we are filthy, mud has gone right through all our clothing and the water runs from off us, a murky brown colour. Fluffy towels and clean clothes before we sit on the bed nursing hot cups of coffee.

Our evening meal is early tonight, the family are having a party to celebrate the baby's three-month anniversary and her return to the family home, or at least that is what we think they are saying! We are invited but decline, they offer us a taste of the party fayre but it does not look that appetising, various bits of pork, liver and some that we could not even identify...

4th January

A good breakfast this morning sets us up for today's shorter walk, and by 9 a.m. we are collected by Phung, our Hmong guide for the day. Phung is not alone; she has her baby strapped to her back – we say strapped but it is more tied in a scarf come sling. Carrying a baby must be a good sign that this walk is going to be easier?

From our hotel it is a steady walk, albeit down a lot of steps into Cat Cat village. The village is set in the Muong Hoa Valley, and famous for its natural beauty, Hmong culture and traditions. Traditional wooden huts line the narrow pathway that wind their way through the village, some of these you can look inside to get a feel for the type of conditions they live in. It is touristy compared to yesterday's walk, stalls selling local handicrafts, homemade corn wine, clothes and souvenirs are dotted around.

There are some lovely waterfalls, alongside the stream are lots of elaborate bamboo waterwheels that use the energy of the water to pound rice. With Mount Fansipan in the distance it truly is a stunning village, and as we leave the wooden huts behind, we meet a buffalo wandering along the path towards us. We push our backs tight into the wall giving it every inch we can to let it past, our Hmong guide Phung is laughing – wondering why we are so nervous of it. Having had our brush with the loose buffalo its pigs and chicken next, animals around here are just left to wander around, all the wood must be used to make houses rather than pens?

We arrive back at our hotel for a late lunch, another great meal, then pack our bags as the bus back to Hanoi leaves at three forty-five. Looking through the windows of the bus, savouring the last of the scenery before darkness falls. There is still time for one refreshment stop as we exit the mountains, and then it is back on our way. We eventually arrive back in Hanoi at 9 p.m., it would have been earlier if the bus had not been stopped by the Police and our driver taken away for half hour or so – no idea what that was all about, but paperwork was being checked, documents produced and what looked like frantic phone calls made...

Back in Hanoi

5th January

Based solely on the number of days, we are now exactly half way through our trip. In reality we have done the largest chunk of our travelling, relaxation is on the horizon for much of our remaining time away. We have a new room on our return to the Indochine Queen 2 Hotel, the shower floods halfway across the bathroom floor, only half the lights work, but apart from that everything is good – including this morning's buffet breakfast, and as if to top that, the sun has come out!

Today we are re-visiting a pair of attractions that we also did in April; this morning we are going to walk out to the Temple of Literature and this afternoon, if we can get tickets, we are going to watch the Water Puppet show by the lake.

The Temple of Literature is dedicated to Confucius and was Vietnams first university, dating back to the eleventh century and is made up of several courtyards and the literature well. They refer to it as a well but it is more a large square pond rather than a well that you would put a bucket down. From its conception in 1076 the royalty and other members of elite society were all taught here, right until its closure in 1779 when the Nguyen dynasty made Hue their capital and founded a 'new' imperial academy.

The layout is based upon the Temple of Qufu in Shandong (China), birthplace of Confucius. In the most simplistic terms Confucianism is a system of thoughts and behaviour; part philosophy, part religion but more with a humanistic way of governing, or way of life more than anything else. Much of what it stands for is still truly relevant today, integrity, honesty, knowledge, justice and humaneness; in a nutshell social harmony and understanding.

Courtyard number three is without doubt the most impressive part, or at least it us for us. As well as having the well in the centre it also has eighty-two 'stelae' of carved stone turtles which honour talent and encourage study. In Confucianism the turtle is a symbol of longevity and wisdom. The stelae are best described as like gravestones that are sat upon the back of a turtle; they are engraved in much the same way. It used to be considered lucky to rub the stone turtles' heads, but a fence has been erected to stop that as it does cause damage.

The fourth courtyard is the ceremonial heart of the complex. The two halls, one on either side, house altars dedicated to the seventy-two most honoured disciples whilst the centre piece is the House of Ceremonies where Confucius himself is worshipped. There is also a museum in here, but in all honesty our minds have already taken in as much as they can for one day, no chance of a turtle wearing a gravestone for us two!

The final courtyard had been destroyed in 1946, during the first Indochina war, so what you see today has all been reconstructed, (as recently as the year 2000). The design of the new fifth courtyard was based on traditional architecture to keep in harmony with the surrounding sights of the temple, but once you know it is only fifteen years old it does lose the sense of awe that the rest of the complex generates within you. We depart feeling enlightened but with our brains frazzled; it is a feast for the eyes even if we will have forgotten all the dates and dynasties referred to by tomorrow morning! Our favourite part was the turtle stelae and you can see why they were inscribed on UNESCO's Memory of the World Register as of historic importance.

We had picked up tickets for the Thanh Long Water Puppet Theatre on our way out to the Temple of Literature, so having had an early shower and change of clothing we are all set for an evening at the theatre! Water puppetry dates all the way back to the eleventh century; when rice paddy fields were flooded villagers would make their own entertainment by standing waist-deep in the water with the puppets performing above the water. In the theatre you don't see the puppeteers at all, they are hidden behind the curtain and using large rods to 'work' the puppets movements.

The puppets are accompanied by an orchestra who play traditional music and sound effects to assist in the drama of the story telling. The shows represent Vietnamese folk tales and legends, often the celebration of the rice harvest but always with a dash of humour. Due to the Thang Long Theatre being so popular with the tourists, rather than one long epic tale, performances are made up of a few short stories. Every show includes the famous 'Legend of the Restored Sword' which enacts the local fable of the giant tortoise in Hoan Kiem Lake that has become a symbol of the city.

It was great to see the show again, the sword story we had remembered from our last visit, other stories were new to us but both entertaining and clever in their telling. Even though you have an idea of how it is all being done you are still puzzled, amazed and in awe of the skill of these puppeteers. For the grand finale you do get to see the people behind the magic; the curtains draw back so they can take their well-deserved round of applause.

6th January

It is our final full day in Vietnam, so after another good breakfast we venture out looking for a souvenir or two as gifts. We have a rough idea of what we are after, the biggest problem is can we find the shops again where we had seen them! They do attractive lacquered gift items, so that is what we are looking for, either decorative plates or vases. By midday it is a case of mission accomplished, so back to the hotel to get them packed safely and juggle our bags around ready for tomorrow's flight.

With it being a nice afternoon, we explore Hoan Kiem lake, visiting the Ngoc Son Temple on the island accessed by the picturesque red bridge. The painted gateways are what first grabs your attention, both before you get to the bridge and once you reach the other side, the bridge represents the rising sun, but there is no sign of that today.

The Temple itself is small but also interesting as there is a small museum as part of the complex too. The name of the lake, Hoan KIem, translates as 'Lake of the Returned Sword' and after last night's puppet re-enactment we finally get the full story of the sword! The legend has it that the emperor had received a magical sword from the Golden Turtle God to chase away the Chinese. Having successfully seen off the Chinese invaders, the emperor is sailing on Hoan Kiem Lake when a giant turtle surfaces and takes the sword from him before disappearing back under the water. The sword was never recovered...

Showered and out to enjoy our last evening in Vietnam we finish off eating where we started, a burger from Lotteria before enjoying a final few beers at our favourite Bia Hoi.

Top row: Sapa Mountains in the sun; Lanterns of Hoi An and Uncle Ho by the Town Hall in Ho Chi Minh City

Middle: Flower sellers in Hanoi, Coracles at An Bang beach (Hoi An) and the Japanese Bridge, Hoi An

Bottom: Us crossing a monkey bridge on the Mekong Delta, Water Puppet Theatre in Hoi An and a soggier Sapa

Vietnam Observations

They are permanently eating, yet somehow remain annoyingly slim.

Clothing sizes are exceedingly small, Alison needs an XXL over here, a size twelve at home!

Pavements are used for everything except for walking on.

Mopeds can be left anywhere; no rules and no restrictions seem to apply.

Locals can sit on the lowest of seats (and get back up again no trouble). They will even take off and sit on their own shoe if no chair is available.

With such small chairs are matching small tables, so no chance of getting your knees tucked under!

Any pavement can become a kitchen or restaurant, and you can bet the food will be delicious.

No health and safety, cooking on open flames in the street, welding with no masks, burning offerings...

You are never more than five minutes away from a donut seller in Hanoi.

Shoe shine is offered even if you are wearing sandals with the smallest straps.

Women work far harder than their male counterparts.

Fantastic crisp varieties, put our salt and vinegar or cheese and onion to shame! Crab Me deserve more recognition in the culinary world.

The only way to get a full-sized chair is to have a haircut!

Bangkok... again!

7th January

Woken at 5:55 a.m. by the phone in our room – our taxi is here! It is not us who are late, it was not due until six thirty. Within ten minutes we are downstairs, reception have kindly packed us a take-away breakfast; we say our goodbyes before being whisked off to the airport. With our bags handed over we buy a coffee, no normal Hanoi prices here, but it is much needed to wake us up properly.

A little turbulence on the flight, and then it is a long queue at Thai immigration before we get the 'A1' bus to the BTS Skytrain station. From there it is a case of making our way to Asoke station, and a short walk to the Amora Neoluxe Hotel to check in there for the second time.

With the sun beating down we take advantage of the rooftop pool and have a lazy afternoon, swimming a few lengths but mainly just being lazy.

A long soak in the bath before we walk to Soi 38 on Sukhumvit Road for something to eat, two green curries and bottles of Chang. Alison is talking to a Thai lady who says that Soi 38, which for years has been synonymous with local street food is to be redeveloped into luxury apartments. That is such a shame as every time we have visited Bangkok it has been our go-to place for eating out; we had better make the most of tonights experience...

8th January

A great night's sleep is followed by an excellent buffet breakfast. Today is our only full day in Bangkok, tomorrow we are back on the move, making our way to Goa with flights that take us via Kuala Lumpur, not the most direct but certainly the most cost efficient.

Planning a second lazy day around the pool we are let down by the weather, so after about an hour we decide to buy day passes for the Skytrain and have one last explore. There is a list of things we need, so currency exchange and a trip to a pharmacy are both on the cards, potentially a book shop to get some reading matter would be handy too.

Rather than following the guidebook completely, we hop off at stations where sights had grabbed our attention, the lesser-known ones that do not merit a mention. Two very nice temples that have a handful of locals making offerings are on a par with much of what we have seen beforehand, there are so many gems scattered around this city. A stop off at the Siam centre is interesting, not cultural in any way but a combination of high-tech shopping mall and entertainment complex; Madame Tussauds, multiplex cinemas and a Sea Life aquarium are just some of the attractions sited here.

Back on the train we head out almost reaching the very end of the line to see the Victory Monument before returning and getting off at Chit Lom for a look at the Erawan Shrine. There is a high police presence around the Shrine, less than six months ago an explosive device left in a backpack had killed twenty visitors and injured dozens more. To us the shrine is not the most spectacular but there is traditional music being played and a dance troupe dressed in traditional costumes moving to it, but more in slow deliberate movements tai chi style.

The shrine has a strange story behind it; the government was building a grand hotel called the Erawan, in Thai culture dates and timings are especially important - unfortunately they had laid the foundations on the wrong day. The construction was delayed repeatedly, cost overruns, injuries and accidents and they even managed to lose a shipload of Italian marble intended for the building. Was there a curse on this development; the Ratchaprasong junction had previously been used to put criminals on public display? Some astrologer suggested building a shrine would help to counter all of these negative influences, so a Brahma statue was designed, built and enshrined in 1956, and from that point onwards the hotels construction continued unhindered!

As we head back to our hotel, we find a second-hand bookshop and get one each to start us off once we arrive in Goa. Fortunately, we like similar books so we can swap around once read. A pack of nuts and broad bean savoury snacks are also taken back to the room for a late afternoon snack.

Determined to make the most of our day passes for the Skytrain we are out early, beers at the Soi Cowboy, and we also discover that it has food stalls early in the evening, could be handy in the future if Soi 38 is no more. We take the Skytrain to Thong Lo and walk the short distance to Soi 38 for what may be our last ever meal down this street, we had better choose wisely. Curried noodles with a chicken on the bone, (that just falls) off and a massaman are the choices for what will also be our last meal in Thailand. One final visit to Patpong, so back on the train to Sala Daeng and a wander up the two streets that make up this world-famous street. Although its best known for the adult-themed bars it also has live music and a night market, so you may be shown leaflets for ping-pong shows whilst browsing a handbag or fake designer clothing...

Goa, India

9th January

This morning will be our last buffet breakfast, from tomorrow we will have the facilities and be making our own, things like washing up, cleaning and stocking fridges will all become part of our new daily routine...

We check out and take the now familiar route via the Skytrain and A1 bus to the Don Muang airport, it all goes smooth and we catch the bus just minutes before it leaves on its half hourly shuttle. Checking in takes an age, and then just as we are being processed a change of shift, no rush as we have seen that our flight has been delayed! Once we are in the departure lounge, we can see that there are military flyovers going on, and later discover that it is to celebrate Thailand's Children Day. That would explain our delay as all flights are being held and rescheduled for an hour later than intended.

Kuala Lumpur airport is much of a blur, having the first part of our flight delayed means that it is now a whistle-stop visit; we follow the transit passenger signs and are soon waiting to board our second flight of the day. This one is a squashed, cramped experience, for some reason Indian passengers always have crazy amounts of hand luggage with them, by the time we board the overhead lockers are full so our hand luggage is wedged under the seats in front.

Welcome to India and the queues for immigration control. Our pen does not write on their forms, yet the books we purchased in Bangkok are covered in bits of scribble – it is not the pen that is faulty! We do manage to borrow a pen from someone else but that is almost as bad, we finally manage to scrawl our details in a very scruffy fashion onto the form. Everyone is having the same issue, dodgy paper... think Izal toilet paper from your schooldays!

Filling in the form was the trickiest part; the bags were already circling on the carousel by the time we got through and our driver was there holding up a name card as we exit the airport building. It is a steady drive to Calangute, North Goa, which will be our home for a little over two months. As we approach the town itself there are signs of life, its approaching midnight by this point so while the restaurants have closed some of the bars are still open.

Valerie, who we have arranged the apartment through has given the keys to our driver, so he is able to lead us straight to the door and let us in. We are located just off the main road, on the ground floor of a small apartment block; exploring inside we are impressed, a spacious living room, good sized bedroom with air-conditioning, kitchen (complete with a washing machine) and a bathroom.

We get into bed, and then have to search for an extra sheet – the air conditioning had been on when we arrived, it obviously works well as the room is a bit on the cool side.

10th January

We sleep well, and although the main road is only fifty metres away, we cannot hear anything at all, it is a cockeral that has brought are sleep to an abrupt end. We make ourselves a coffee and figure out the washing machine, it is obviously brand new as it still has all the labels on, but it loads from the top. We have no powder but run through a wash of essentials regardless, we do have a small veranda with a washing line accessed from the door in our bedroom.

Alison does like a list, so is in her element creating our first shop. In the kitchen we also have a fridge with a small freezer compartment at the top, a two-ring gas stove and a kettle, so cooking for ourselves is now an option. Cleaning products also need to be on our first shop, washing up liquid, wash powder, a small scrubbing brush etc. Overall, we are more than satisfied with what we have got.

We go out onto the main road and realise exactly where we are, a perfect location for us as our favourite bar, Madhu's, is just a hundred metres or so to the right. Walking down the road the other way, to the left is the Calangute roundabout, we pass the Lambada Hotel where we have stayed before and recognise a lot of the restaurants that we have eaten in, it is like coming home!

Our shopping list is all to no avail, the supermarkets are not open on a Sunday, so our plans are shelved until tomorrow. We head back along the Baga road towards our apartment, which we now realise is situated just behind the Union Bank of India, and Valerie has her travel agency / money exchange in a small office that is also part of that block.

We head into Madhu's where we are greeted enthusiastically by the guys who run it, we have been regulars in here for a good number of years and just love the simplicity of the place; plastic tables and chairs, cold beer and friendly staff. It is the perfect place to people watch and enjoy the chaos that is Indian life. A tradition of ours from holidays past is that our first meal is always at Mirabai's, and always the same; it goes back years from when I ate the best curry I have ever eaten, their red chilli chicken. Unfortunately, over the years they have tweaked it and it has never reached the dizzy heights of that first occasion since. Alison goes for the vindaloo and we share the two dishes between us, a definite thumbs up but lacking a bit of the fiery heat that we hoped for!

On our way back to our apartment we are intercepted by an elderly couple, they had seen us leaving this morning and it turns out that they are Valerie's Mum and Dad, Esme and Michael. We introduce ourselves; Michael is a huge cricket fan and Esme loves cooking – over the next few weeks we get to sample a few of her dishes!

Our afternoon is spent sorting through our luggage, we finally have a wardrobe to hang things up in, the remainder of the dirty washing is left in the bags awaiting washing powder. We bring in the sweeping brush from the veranda and run that around the place, the mopping will also have to wait until we have cleaning products. Flicking through TV channels we are delighted to see that we have Star Sports, so we will be able to catch up on the football. Having watched the early kick-off we get ready to go out, only to find out that we have minimal hot water, well minimal water. We manage a quick wash before heading to Krishna's for our tea, two curry meals in one day – we will end up huge if we keep this up!

We pop back to Madhu's and are pleased to see that a local character, Chef, is sat in his usual seat, there are also a lot of other faces we recognise from previous years – we are not the only creatures of habit! Service has improved, ice is readily available whereas other years tracking down the ice bucket used to be a case for Inspector Morse. We get chatting to Chef, everyone refers to him as that as he is a fantastic cook and makes pies for some of the local restaurants and customers of Madhu's. He also does a range of cookies that have his special magical ingredient... It turns out that he has had an eventful year, and not in a good way, not only had he the misfortune to fall and broke his hip but he had also been arrested for possession of one of the key elements to his cookies! There is never a dull moment when the Chef is around...

11th January

There is still no water when we turn the taps on first thing. At least we have some bottled water so can still make coffee. A knock on the door and the whirlwind that is Valerie comes in, full of hugs and welcomes. She is looking very well, happy that we like the apartment and pleased to see us, as we are her. It is a flying visit as she has her shop to open, we say that we will pop in a little later to catch up with her husband Savio and their daughter Sovann too.

A trip to the nearby supermarket fulfils half of our shopping list, a trip to one of the bigger stores will be needed too. Heading off into town we soon track down the missing items in the Bombay Bazaar; on our return home we can now sweep and mop the floor, water has been restored! Another load of washing done and hung out before we head down to the beach, but not before stopping at the Infantaria for lunch. Infantaria, is part bakery, part restaurant – but serves fantastic food and snacks. We opt for a mix of quiches, samosas and egg chops (like scotch eggs, but spicier).

Our afternoon is spent on the beach, we walk down the Calangute steps, turning left until we reach the Rovers Return beach shack. The sun is not too hot, or its more the case that the breeze is keeping us cool. We have a drink and people watch, there is always beach sellers trying to make a living but also with one eye out for the local plod who will confiscate all their goods given half a chance. There is not much you cannot buy; speakers, fruit, massage, shawls, clothing, drums, maps, watches – if it can be carried then it can be sold on the beach.

We return home, visiting Valerie on the way back, we have some money to collect from her. Savio and Sovann are both looking well and we cannot believe how Sovann has grown since we last see her; unfortunately, we have no English chocolate for her on this occasion!

Food wise we try somewhere new tonight, Chick and Fish on the main road, chosen as much because it looked busy. The chicken cafreal and chicken chilli fry were both tasty and spice laden. We will certainly eat here again. Back in Madhu's we have a prime slot, the tables right at the front mean that you can then rest your feet on the wall! It is not long before a couple we have met the other year arrive, we have a bit of a chat but they are out with another couple tonight – we will get a proper catch up another night...

12th January

The first Honey Bee (local brandy) hangover, we are both suffering this morning! Nothing that cannot be worked through, an additional cup of coffee sees it off.

Another trip to the supermarket in Calangute, tea, sugar, rice and some spice mixes; getting set for cooking our own meals some evenings. A visit to the 'chicken shop', or Royals as its nameboard says, it sells chickens and not much else, legs, mince, breasts, whole... if its chicken Royals will have it. They sell eggs too. Returning through the market and we pick up some bananas, we are laden down by now, so the vegetables that we need will have to wait until tomorrow.

The afternoon is again spent on the beach, the sea is pretty rough and Alison is hanging onto her bottoms as she comes back up after being completely knocked off her feet by a wave! The waves are great fun but tiring, it really is a job to keep your footing as they crash over you. Walking back home we pick up some samosas and batatawadas from the guy who sets up daily outside the Red Lion Pub at around four o' clock, wrapped up in newspaper they will keep warm to eat with a nice cup of tea. It turns out that what we thought was sugar isn't, once we have Wi-Fi Google translate tells us that it is a vitamin supplement.

On the topic of Wi-Fi; whilst it is everywhere and easily accessible in Cambodia and Vietnam it is not so easy to come by, or the reliability as good, here in Goa. It seems strange as everyone automatically thinks of India as the world leader for out-sourced call centres, perhaps we need to buy ourselves a SIM card for the data package? For this evening though, we need to find a connection - we have a drink in the Cricketers, but sadly their Wi-Fi is no good. Our next try is more successful, Mirabai's for a meal, the prawn vindaloo is divine, and even more so when the owner of the restaurant recommends adding a few chopped onions and lime juice, beautiful! The Wi-Fi connection in here is also good, so we can catch up with emails, check in on home etc.

A Kingfisher beer or two in Madhu's round off this evening, Chef is sat in there and he has brought us his price list – a good old pie will be on our dinner plates before too long...

13th January

We are both as fit as fiddles this morning, the early night has done us some good. As we venture out Valerie is putting her boards out, advertising her excursions and currency exchange rates. We tell her about our shopping expedition yesterday and she 'tells' us that she will give us a cooking lesson, 12:30 p.m. tomorrow – and that if we pop back in later, she will have a list of ingredients we will need. We take the opportunity to ask if the apartment owner could get us a toaster, our breakfast options are a bit limited!

Over the years I have bought leather slip on sandals from the same guy who sells them on Beach Road, we spotted him on our way back from the sea front yesterday. They are some of the comfiest that I have ever had and the quality is exceptionally good too, today I am hopeful of buying a new pair. He remembers us, and he has the usual style that I go for, a straightforward slip on, nothing between the toes as I find that uncomfortable. That is me easily sorted, price negotiated and bought. Alison sees some that she likes but just not in her size – hers will have to be especially made and be ready for collection in a few days!

As we go down the lane by Valerie's shop, she comes out brandishing not only a shopping list but also a toaster for us, unfortunately it has a crack in it; so close to getting a cooked breakfast! Valerie advises us that the horn we hear each night around six thirty is the bread man making his deliveries, if you pop out to him you can buy fresh pav buns, that sounds like a plan. With that in mind we pop to the little supermarket nearby and buy a bag of eggs, no such thing as cartons here, just a little see-through polythene bag.

With cooking ourselves tomorrow we don't order any pies from Chef, instead we opt for his home-made pate, another breakfast option, once we have that toaster! A few beers ensue and a small bottle of the Honey Bee brandy...

14th January

Breakfast, wow! Fried eggs in buttery pav buns and a splash of tomato sauce, simplistic but heavenly. The yolks are bright orange, free range is standard here and the tomato sauce has subtle spicing to it rather than our version.

We have plenty of chicken from our shopping the other day, the rest of the list means a trip to the market, onions, tomatoes and potatoes. We smile as the lady at the market put all three items on the scales together, rather than weigh them individually like you would at home. Total price is forty rupees, so with the current exchange rate forty pence – converting prices is so easy when you get so near to one hundred rupees to the pound!

Half past twelve and Valerie arrives at our apartment, not empty-handed either – a toaster! Our cookery lesson is not only entertaining but also a great learning curve; we both cook at home but there is an enormous difference between following a recipe and being shown by a particularly good cook of exactly how to treat the spices to get the best flavour. Today's lesson will cover a vegetable pilau rice, chicken vindaloo and a riata dip, Valerie makes everything look so easy, from the chopping and dicing all the way through to the cooking, and with what we would count as limited equipment. The smells are making us hungry, cannot wait to eat that this evening!

After cleaning everything up afterwards, washing up etc, we pop out for a couple of beers – it got ridiculously hot in that kitchen! Sitting by the wall with our feet up, drinking ice-cold Kingfisher, does life get much better this? The road in front of us is getting busier, during the week its mostly scooters and taxis, today there are plenty of big four by four cars that are negotiating their way past all the obstacles, think cows, dogs, tourists... Goa is extremely popular with domestic tourists at weekends and on public holidays; it is so different to any other Indian state, far more relaxed and liberal than the rest of the country – they all flock here to let their hair down and party! The festival of Makara Sankranti celebrates the Hindu sun god Surya, meaning a public holiday, and it seems that many have booked extra days off to take full advantage of it

It is the time of day where we switch the television on; while reheating the feast that we helped cook this afternoon we watch MasterChef Asia, the last few days have had us hooked, hopefully something we can learn from watching that too. Our meal is delicious, on a par with restaurant food, we would love to be able to cook that well ourselves. The vegetable pilau is more than just a rice accompaniment, it is a great tasting dish, and there will be some of that left over for tomorrow.

15th January

Fried egg buns again for breakfast, and a big clean up.

We are not untidy by any means, pots are always washed and dried, but it is the sand – it gets everywhere! A thorough sweep up and mop should stop us trailing it into our bed, plus I give the bathroom a once over too. The bathroom is more a wet room, so with a slight turn of the shower head you could wash while sitting on the toilet! A lip of a centimetre is all that separates the toilet and the basin from the shower section, so the water bounces off your body and then drains back, leaving the sand behind. Each day we swill the sand away but it is a constant battle...

With jobs done we head down to the beach, at the foot of the Calangute steps the beach is heaving with Indian visitors. They are having a fun time – the vendors hiring out the jet-skis and parasailing experiences must be raking it in. What makes us smile is that the Indian ladies venture in the sea wearing their saris, very few Indian men have proper swimming gear either, stripping down to their pants is classed as beach-ready!

I guess living in the UK most of us grow up experiencing days on the beach through our childhood? For many Indians a beach is a new experience, and fair play to them, the inner child comes out; they play the games we all did growing up, burying each other in the sand seems to be the favourite! We have a lazy few hours, a dish of spiced chips at the Rovers Return and a couple of lime sodas before heading back up beach road towards home. No sign of the shoe seller today, and we are too early for the samosa guy so a bag of Masala Munch crisps for an afternoon snack today – along with what remains of the vegetable pilau!

Tonight's meal is at another one of our favourite restaurants when we are in Goa, though we normally only visit the once, on the last evening before a flight home. The Tibetan Kitchen does a fantastic beef steak, with crushed potatoes and a delicious side salad; it tasted every bit as good as before but a little pricier than we recalled, never mind it is an attractive setting for a bit of a treat. Like most evenings we finish off in Madhu's, Chef has brought us a tub of the pate we had ordered – so after a couple of beers we go home, fire up the toaster and share a sample slice between us...

16th January

Every Saturday there is a local market where you can buy almost anything. It is the fruit and vegetables that we have gone for - but if we had wanted padlocks, shoelaces, jeans or towels we would have been successful too. The prices are incredibly low, even for our white faces! We buy some more spices, bananas and strawberries, the rest of the vegetables we will pick up from the covered market, purely because it is closer to home and less of a distance to carry.

Our afternoon is spent cooking, another chicken vindaloo, Bombay spuds (more by my recipe from at home). Alison creates a riata as a dip and a vegetable pilau rice, but the texture is not as good as the Valerie assisted attempt though. We have done bigger portions this time, with plenty of live football on we can eat at home, save costs and enjoy the match while we eat. There is enough food here for both Saturday and Sunday.

With our earlier cooking reheated and dished up we get sat down and watch the first game. The food is an enormous success, and whilst the vegetable rice does not have the fluffy texture it is still very palatable! Our plans to watch the second game are interrupted by a lack of cable signal, so it is an early night with a book.

17th January

Even though we have only been here a week we have already settled into some kind of routine; days at the beach are interspersed with a shopping and then cooking day, a morning spent cleaning or an afternoon walk. From a diary point of view, it would get very repetitive and boring...

So how would we describe Goa, or more specifically Calangute? A quick history lesson immediately explains why Goa is so different from the rest of India; so, briefly and in simplistic terms, Britain ruled over India from 1858, making it part of the British Empire, Goa had already been colonised by the Portuguese over four centuries earlier and Britain had no interest in causing any upheaval, so just left well alone.

The influence of Portugal on Goa meant that Christianity was the main religion and way of life, everywhere else in India mainly fell under either Hinduism or Islam (before partition), and this is what differentiates Goa from the rest of the country. We have travelled around India a lot over the years and they are like two different worlds, so much of what attracts tourists to Goa just would not be accepted in most of the country.

Calangute itself is in the north of Goa, and part of the three small towns that make up the hive of activity of the Candolim – Calangute – Baga tourist mecca. If you are feeling energetic you can walk between them along the beach or the road that joins the three together. Candolim is the quieter of the three, Calangute, for us at least gives a happy medium, whilst Baga is where it is all at if you fancy a really late night (early hours of the morning), clubbing or mixing with the local youngsters.

Demographic wise, the visitors from the UK tend to be older, although we have noticed that younger people seem to have discovered it in the last few years and the average age must be coming down! Our first visit took us by surprise, lots of retirees with fantastic tans and shiny white teeth! As well as enjoying winter sunshine many have full health check-ups, opticians and any dental work done, all at a fraction of the price back home.

North Goa has some lovely sandy beaches, but I do not think anyone would call it paradise. What it does have though is such friendly people, the Goan people are so welcoming and they play a big part in what attracts people back year after year. Some of the other obvious benefits are almost constant sunshine between November and April, your money goes a lot further than anywhere in Europe, the food is fantastic and alcohol and nights out are far more affordable than back at home.

That has listed all the good points... The downsides are that it is not very clean, India still has a massive issue with litter. Many visitors refer to Goa as 'Paradise in a Dustbin', and it is hard to disagree, maybe the next generation of Goans will make a difference? For us it is also getting too touristy, while Cambodia and Vietnam have very much kept their own way of doing things Goa (or at least North Goa), now has karaoke bars and bingo nights – we much prefer to just people watch and take in their way of life. The other side of that coin is that you can get a fantastic Sunday lunch, roast beef, Yorkshire pud, the works...

the rest of January

Breakfast has turned into a daily fried egg in a pav bun (more on the pav bun in a little while). The toaster is getting plenty of use too, and Chef's pate is a regular treat!

Alison got her new hand-made shoes collected from the guy on Beach Road, they fit perfectly. Wi-Fi, or at least access continues to be a pain at most places, we have a couple of 'go to' places so that we are still managing to stay connected with everyone back home.

We've both had haircuts, a tiny shop on the Baga road, about eye-level to the road once you have gone down the steps, I go first and he does a great job for the 100 rupees. Alison is that impressed that the following day she pays the same for a trim herself, she did have a couple of beers beforehand to steady her nerves though!

Other discoveries include Infantarias apple pie and ice cream; heavenly, big chunks of apple, lightly spiced with cinnamon and the creamiest ice cream you can imagine... We have a new favourite dish, Hyderabad biriyani; we often order this instead of a rice dish and then we go for a naan instead. Paneer, absolutely love it – just not something we had considered in the past.

On the days when we visit the food market, we have taken to having lunch at the Café Anan, a proper locals place with prices to match. We have Valerie to thank for the tip as we would never have considered it otherwise. We have two of each; samosas, batatawadas, egg chops, cups of chai and cake, all for ninety-four rupees, less than one pound.

A Sunday dinner at the Rovers Return was a taste of home, it is so popular that you must book a time slot. It did seem strange sitting on the beach eating a full roast dinner but it compared well to pub lunches that we have had at home. If we were to be overly fussy, the mash potato was sloppier than we like, but otherwise it was brilliant.

Cooking for ourselves we have been making pav bhaji, pav being the bun and bhaji being nothing like an onion bhaji! The packet mix of that name is added to tomatoes, onions, grated carrots, peas, potatoes, so in English terms the vegetables are all cooked together and then mashed, so a spicy mashed potato fusion served in a warm bun... In addition to our home cooking, we sometimes get food parcels from Valerie's Mum, no wonder our clothes are shrinking...

Prawns... absolutely massive compared to what we get at home! Valerie orders them and then we pay her for them, like most things in Goa a white face pays far more than a local. We are given a quick lesson in preparing them and some masala (blend of spices) to cook them in, really, really tasty. Prawns are not something we eat much of at home as they are so expensive, it feels like we are spoiling ourselves!

The pav buns... it turns out the breadman has been ripping us off! By chance we happen to be in Valeries shop when the breadman passes by, Valerie orders from him and gets seven pav buns for her twenty rupees; he has been charging us ten rupees each – you should get three for that! We are not sure what Valerie said to him, but the next night he was very sheepish, and we are charged correctly from that day on.

It is while sitting in Madhu's one afternoon that we can now say beyond all doubt, Indian women work far harder than their male counterparts... Roadworks are going on right outside, no mechanical equipment, no shoes either - just pickaxes and shovels. The man has taken charge of leaning on the shovel while the woman is left to wield the pickaxe, she is striking blow after blow while he just shovels every once in a while, just to keep it clear for her! We had noticed on another night women do all the carrying, if their hands are full some will balance stuff on their heads - while the bloke walks behind emptyhanded...

Most evenings we end up in Madhu's, exceeding our alcohol units each week. I have moved onto the Old Monk rum while Alison sticks to the Honey Bee, a can of coke suits us both as the mixer. We catch up with friends from previous years; Mike and Sylvia rent an apartment just outside of Calangute, so travel in each evening on their scooter. Somehow Sylvia still manages to look immaculate despite having worn a helmet – she did use to be a hairdresser, expert knowledge?

With no live music and with tables limited, we often share with others, you get to meet some interesting people and the strangest of conversations. The drinks flow, spirits are bought by the bottle, albeit 180 millilitres sized ones. Your bill is tallied up at the end, calculated from your empties; by the end of the night your table is full of empty cans, maybe a couple of empty beer bottles and occasionally two empty spirit bottles each. We never had a bill that cost more than six pounds, you cannot get a drink each for that at home in many places! Unsurprisingly there has been the odd hangover...

Early to Mid-February

The month starts badly, SpiceJet have changed our flight schedule for Varanasi, their change means that we now arrive in Delhi late in the afternoon but do not depart for Varanasi until the next morning – nightmare! Valerie comes to our rescue, no doubt it helps that she is a booking agent, but by the end of the day we have better flights than our original booking! Rather than flying via Delhi we now transit through Hyderabad, the waiting around time is good too, comfortable rather than tight!

G and M Jewellers has a fantastic reputation, so going on that we walk out towards Baga and Alison takes her rings for a combination of repair, replate and polish; one for each. The price seems very reasonable at just under ten pounds for all that work. We are slightly worried at leaving that amount of value with him, I guess back at home a jewellers would have insurance in place in case of loss or damage? Fingers crossed...

Walking past the Casa Aleixo, a place where we have stayed at before, we meet Mr. Wilfred whose family home it is. Built in a traditional Portuguese style it is our favourite place to stay when in Goa, it sits back nicely from the road, has a small swimming pool and Mr. Wilfred is an interesting guy. We are not sure how old he and his wife are, past retirement age we suspect, but he still has his finger in many business pies! They are a lovely couple and very selective of who gets to stay in their home, luckily, he seems to like us! He says to pop in at some point before we leave, we will take him up on that.

The jewellers did an amazing job, what were we worrying about? They really do look like new, the one that was repaired now looks in pristine condition. He does try upselling as we collect them, Alison's eyes light up but we do leave with nothing. As the jeweller shows, most people can be trusted, not all though; every two or three weeks I send a postcard home to Mum and Dad, on the third occasion the cashier at the post office tries too hugely overcharge us for a stamp – it was like 'pavgate' all over again!

It is rare we leave the apartment before ten in the morning, USA MasterChef has become addictive, it is far more cut throat than our version and has interesting twists along the way. Sometimes one contestant will get less time to cook, or perhaps his other competitors choose his ingredients, knowing his weaknesses – it does keep it more interesting.

A remarkably close encounter with a cow got our hearts pumping one morning! Walking side by side this cow come charging around the corner at full speed and passes right between us; this bovine was far nimbler than we thought possible, for that split second it seemed like it had to hit us!

Our days on the beach are still enjoyable, in the past our attention span means that within an hour or two we are bored. Second hand bookshops have been the key to our beach success, a constant supply of reading material means that we are quite content on the sunbeds. Some days we spend a lot of time in the sea, others it is just too rough; I am ok with drawstring trunks, Alison is in danger of indecency charges – crashing waves have no respect for dignity, top half or bottom...

The shacks provide sunbeds free of charge, they make their living from guests eating and drinking there – fair enough. We opt for food at midday, a light snack to keep us going, but sometimes a breakfast too. They make fantastic milkshakes, sell beer obviously and plenty of water to rehydrate, we are spending six hours there some days, putting a proper shift in!

Alison is so impressed with her hand-made shoes that she orders a second pair, for leather sandals you just cannot go wrong, they wear well and are as comfortable as slippers. Not to be left out I treat myself to a new sunhat, the one from Vietnam is so faded and stained by sweat. As well as 'shoe man' also on the route back from the beach is the Red Lion, if we get to that point before 'samosa man' we sometimes stop for a beer. One large bottle of Kingfisher between the two of us means that it is drank before it gets too warm, we can soon order a second ice cold one! The samosa stall does not take long to fire up, so we can then head home by half past four with a snack that will keep us full until our evening meal.

Cooking wise we are improving, for the first time ever I have cooked a decent biriyani, that has always been my Achilles heel, I am over the moon with that. Valerie drops in various food parcels, not always Indian either, cheese filled potato croquets on one occasion. Esme sends us fish dishes around; she obviously doesn't think we are starving because she happily points out that we are packing the weight on! Add into the mix occasional pies from the Chef, and pate too, we are living very well.

We discover different routes into town, rather than going via the main road and up to the roundabout we can continue along the track behind our apartment. The proper road soon gives out to a sandy, dusty track, concrete buildings turn into tarpaulin and tin-roofed living quarters, to be honest it takes us a little by surprise, we have seen such builds in other parts of India but not in Goa, one of Indias wealthiest states.

As well as learning a new route to town we also discover new words. Chana, as in a chana masala means chickpea – I did go hungry that day, Alison had to eat the whole lot as I cannot stand them! Café Anan has no descriptions by the dishes, just the local name – so the only way to find out is by ordering one, on the plus side the cake we had also ordered was now all mine...

A tea bag crisis takes some resolving, for some reason we cannot find any anywhere! Loose tea is on sale by the bucket load, and its two full days before we track the bagged variety down. It is while on the great tea bag hunt that we see our first scooter prang, for this trip I had got an International Driving Permit, planning to hire a moped so we could explore further. Once we arrived in Goa and see the chaos on the roads, we promptly dismissed that idea, it is just not the right place for someone with no experience.

Two days of cold water, I switch the heater on and the trip switch blows, Savio resets it but it immediately trips again. The next day we wait in for an electrician who pronounces it as dead, he will fit a replacement in the morning! The new water heater certainly creates more heat than the last one, not that we shower in anything more than lukewarm.

Evenings are more of the same; if we have not cooked ourselves, we are alternating between a handful of restaurants - Carvalhos, Chick and Fish, Krishna, Mirabai's and the Kindman. The Kindman is known for its pork chops and more English style food, but we love it for its chicken vindaloo, they do not hold back on the heat! Most evenings we sit and chat with Mike and Sylvia in Madhu's, they are always good company and share the same sense of humour. Sylvia even convinces us that Feni, the local alcohol brew isn't as bad as we remember, served long with lemonade it is rather nice...

Valerie, Savio and Sovann take us out for a meal too, a restaurant called Fortunes that is out of town. We all squeeze into Savios car and make the short journey away from the coast (we are not sure where, but certain we travel inland!). The food is outstanding, the chicken cafreal is one we have never tried before, but from now on is added to our list of regular choices. The coated fried mussels were something else that we would never order either, they know what dishes are good and it is an opportunity for us to try new foods, knowing it won't be wasted if we don't like it.

Late February

Oman Air have changed the first leg of our flight home, meaning that we do not arrive in Oman before the second leg departs. The solution they offer us is to put us up for the night in Muscat, and then make the second flight the following day. We are quite happy with their proposal, but need to email the taxi company back home – does collecting us from Heathrow on a Sunday rather than a Saturday double the fare that they have given us? Hopefully they will be prompt in getting back to us.

On the food front, chai kulfi (tea flavoured ice-cream). Something else we discovered on the walk back from the beach; before if we had an ice-cream we had gone with the 'Qwality Walls' bike sellers, the same Walls brand from back home. The kulfi sellers are more independents, no fancy trolley bikes, just a huge tub mounted on the back and a scoop, but so creamy and tasty.

An evening meal discovery is the Rock Café, or more precisely, their steaks. Nothing fancy, a chunk of steak and chips; as much as we both love curry there is a breaking point where you fancy something more familiar!

Our taxi company are happy to collect us on the Sunday for the same price, so we email Oman Air back confirming that we are happy with their suggestion. In fact, we are delighted, hoping that a full night's sleep between the two flights should help us avoid suffering from jet lag?

We have a catch up with Wilfred at the Casa Aleixo, he is looking very well. He invites us in for drinks on the terrace with a group of ladies that he has stopping over, from what we gather they are old friends, some from Mumbai and others from Delhi but they meet up in Goa occasionally. They are all very chatty and interesting company; Wilfred is full of it in host mode and keeps the beers flowing. After an hour or so we make our excuses, and leave him in the company of the ladies...

Valerie and Savio invite us for a meal at their home, along with another English couple who they are good friends with. Savio kindly picks us up and takes us to their apartment in Para Towers, from what we see it looks a very modern development and their place is lovely. Some of their church families are also there and it is a great evening of excellent food and interesting conversation. We are not religious in any way, and fortunately the evening was not too heavy or didn't get uncomfortable for us. Whilst they sang praise the

English contingent sat it out on the balcony, but a great night and good to share different opinions and experiences.

Varanasi

27th February

Varanasi. One of the oldest continually inhabited cities in the world, and by this evening we will be there. For anyone who is fascinated by India then they will already know a lot about this holy place, we have seen programme after programme on it, but now we are going to get to experience it for ourselves.

Our usual breakfast and then a quick tidy up before the taxi arrives to collect us. As usual we check about a dozen times that we have our passports and tickets that Valerie has printed off for us. Collected on time and dropped off at Goa airport within the same hour, the day has started smoothly and continues that way, no flight delays. There is no luggage for us to check in so we are soon through to the departure lounge, and before we know it, we are on the short walk to our awaiting plane...

Today we are to board a Bombardier Q400 – and it has no jets just a propeller! It seems so small; boarding is at the rear where the stairs become part of the plane once it has been folded back up, and at just 78 seats, two either side of the aisle it seems tiny. I must admit I was nervous, but once in the air it was a smooth journey – landing was a bit rougher but overall, I enjoyed the experience.

The changeover in Hyderabad runs on time and we are soon boarding onto a more standard plane. Just like the first flight we are the only white faces onboard, lots of children mean it is not the quietest or most relaxing flight! To complete the experience sprinkle in a bout of turbulence that delayed the meal service, we were well ready to get off by the time we arrived in Varanasi. With no luggage to collect or passport control with it being a domestic flight we are soon heading towards the exit.

A driver arranged by the Baba Guesthouse is already waiting for us as we leave the airport building, but before we can set off, he must search for the driver of a car who has blocked him in! It only delays our journey for a few minutes before we set off with Bangla music playing on the car stereo. He tells us his name is Babaloo but we do not think he knows many words of English. As we approach the city it is crazy, yes, we have hit rush hour; cars, cows, motorbikes, cycles – you name it, everything is jockeying for position and not prepared to give an inch! It takes an hour to crawl through the last couple of miles before he pulls over and phones the Guesthouse for someone to collect us.

It takes five minutes for him to get here, we climb out and he tells us to follow him... We are led down a warren of small alleys, dodging bikes, cow dung and cows; these alleys are tight, there is no way to give them a wide berth, you are literally brushing up each other. For the first time on our travels the question 'what have we done?' goes through our mind, this place is daunting – how will we ever find our way around these mazes on our own?

After what seemed like an age, we reach the Baba Guesthouse and are given a welcome cup of chai while we get checked in, the sweetness of the chai must be good for our shock. Our room is compact but clean, the bathroom is really nice. We ask about food but none is available; we do not fancy venturing out; its dark by now and we are not convinced we would find our way back, so we finish the rest of our biscuits. Tonight, is going to be an exceedingly early night, we get cosy under our furry blanket, hoping against hope we can evade the mosquitoes...

28th February

A new morning and we wake with a more positive mindset. We had both slept well and somehow not been eaten alive! It is still quite early, before eight anyway, and we have no breakfast option here at the Baba Guesthouse, so off we go.

The first corner we turn and there is a restaurant, also called Baba, how handy is that - if only we had known last night! We order parathas, curd and chai, it will at least start us off for the day. As we sit and eat our breakfast a cow wanders by, pauses and looks in at us, as if it were considering a meal itself. We settle our bill and say 'Ghats?', they seem to understand and point which way we want to be – back past our guesthouse...

The first turn after our guesthouse and we get our first glimpse of the Ganges and within a minute, after stepping over several sleeping dogs, we are on Munshi Ghat. The word ghat means a series of steps leading down to water, Varanasi is made up of eighty-eight of them; many of them form one long continuous promenade, so you can walk a good distance and take in daily life on the Ganges.

This is the Holiest of all places for Hindus, to die and have your funeral here is their life's wish. They believe that the Ganges River is the most holy of rivers and for their ashes to be immersed here is the ultimate salvation. We are not walking for long at all before we reach one of the burning ghats, Harishchandra; in the distance, closer to the river is a shrouded body on a bed of wood, waiting to be set alight. It is too early in the morning to be taking any of that in so we continue our walk.

Further along we arrive at a bathing ghat; a mix of men, women and children are all going through their morning rituals. On a wall by the steps a mirror is propped up as ladies do their hair, on the steps barbers are giving haircuts and shaves to their customers, no disposable razors, cut throat ones rinsed in a bucket of water. It actually feels quite intrusive just being here, it is hard to imagine going through your daily hygiene routine in full view of the passing world.

Next ghat along, more bathers – only this time it is a herd of buffalo. Their herder is in the river with them and he is giving them a good brushing, and they look like they are really enjoying it! Its barely gone nine thirty and our minds are already blown; yes, we have seen it on the TV but to witness it with your own eyes is something else, within a hundred or so metres there are bodies being burnt, buffalo's bathing and in-between the two, bath time for the local residents before they head out to work...

We double-back on ourselves and walk back towards where we started, and then continue beyond that until we reach the main burning ghat. This one looks a lot more formal; the wood neatly stacked at the top of the steps, right by the side of a massive sets of scales. Some Indian guy shows us to the viewing platform and explains a bit more about the process – who gets cremated here, how the type of wood shows your place in society, likewise the proximity to the river of where you are cremated. It is all interesting stuff, but we know his hand will be held out for a tip within minutes...

From the viewing platform we see body after body laid out on frames, like wooden stretchers. They are all covered in a shroud, awaiting their turn to be washed in the Ganges before being set alight in front of the male family members, and subsequently having their ashes taken away by the river. The funeral pyres along the ghats burn constantly, day and night - you can only look on at a respectful distance with awe, for the deceased and their family this is what they have always wanted.

After some banana pancakes at Spicey Bites we carry on walking along the steps by the river, there are a lot of people about, boat trips whilst the sun is setting is what they are all selling and we negotiate a price for an hour trip later in the day. Weddings are also extremely popular here; we have seen at least five already – part of their ritual also involves a blessing from the Ganges. They do seem to like a decorated horse for the wedding, they can be hired just like we would a limousine. We never see anyone on the horse so not sure what part they play on the big day...

The sunset boat cruise is good, the towering buildings of the ghats in a range of styles slowly obscure the setting sun, leaving a reddish glow behind them. It is also the most auspicious time to be cremated, the Manikarnika Ghat has at least twelve pyres alight as we sail past at a respectable distance, the whole steps are just covered in patches of orange flames and shrouded in black smoke. The young rower who took us out was a great guide, pointing out various sights and telling us about the meaning of the Aaarti ceremony on the Dashashwamedh ghat that we are going to see next.

Aarti is a ritual displaying devotion by using fire as an offering. The recipient of the offering is the Goddess Ganga, affectionately sometimes referred to as Ma Ganga, the goddess of the holiest river in India. The Aarti takes place every sunset near the Kashi Vishwanath Temple without fail. We had seen them washing the plates and fancy lamps in the river this afternoon, not really knowing what they were, perhaps they were table adornments from a local restaurant had gone through our heads! They do look a bit like those fancy cake stands that your Nan used to have.

To a backdrop of drumming the devotees draped in saffron coloured robes spread out the plates and lamps before them. The blowing of a conch shell signals the start and the wafting of incense and the circling of the large flaming lamps begins. It is a noisy affair, but the sandalwood from the sticks is pleasant, they are the ones that we always take home! We stay and watch for half hour; in all honesty we are not spiritual people and it is very repetitive – but at least we can say that we witnessed it. It is amazing just how many people have hired boats to view the ceremony from the water rather than the wooden benches, never seen so many rowing boats at one time, hundreds of them!

While the crowds are still watching the Aarti, we head off back to Spicey Bites, vegetarians for the night as we order a chilli paneer and a cashew nut curry. What a day, and to round it off perfectly we find our way back to the Baba guesthouse without getting lost at all...

29th February

We slept well, awoken by the sounds of monkeys running by our window, and across the tin roofs below, not an everyday experience!

After a leisurely breakfast, same place as yesterday, we make the short journey through the narrow alleyways and onto the ghats. Our destination is the Assi Ghat, the southernmost one within the city, but also one of the largest, extremely popular with tourists, due to its proximity to the Monkey Temple. The walk is beyond where we ventured too yesterday, so on route we pass the bathers, buffaloes and bodies awaiting cremation on the Harishchandra ghat.

It is only our second day here in Varanasi and as daft as it may seem, the shock of seeing the bodies, albeit covered in a shroud, no longer phases us – it is just what happens here, all day every day. This morning there seems to be more pyres lit and in the brief time it takes us to pass by, we see two more bodies being carried down the steps towards the river. It appears to us that locals make a living by accosting visitors and telling them about what they are seeing, this ghat will take the deceased of any religion apart from Islam... that is all we learnt as we continued our walk making our excuses before he could ask for his tip!

Assi ghat is a hive of activity; more boat trips for sale, snake charmers, ice-cream sellers, tuk-tuk drivers and cycle-rickshaws all wanting to take you somewhere. We watch a snake charmer for a short while before heading up the steps and going off in search of the Durghar Temple, often referred to as the Monkey Temple due to the sheer number of them wandering around it! We ask directions, more than once, but are getting nowhere, the advice we are given often contradicts what the last person said! With cycle-rickshaws in plentiful supply we hail one down and ask for a price, it seems reasonable to us so we jump aboard.

What follows is a lot longer journey than we were expecting, the guidebook describes it as minutes away from Assi ghat (hence why we were planning on walking), but at least it is not us doing the pedalling... When we finally reach our destination, we are dropped off at the Sankat Mochan Hanuman Temple, our driver points across at it, saying monkey, monkey. The penny drops with us, Hanuman is the Hindu monkey god, or at least depicted in that way, so where we wanted to go to was lost in translation! Now we are here we take a quick look around, before promptly getting a tuk-tuk to the correct one. One thing we have learned from this episode is that these Indian cycle-rickshaw wallahs work extremely hard for their money!

Durghar Temple is not the most attractive one we have ever seen; it is painted a deep brick red for starters! We discover more about it, of its importance to the Hinduism religion and how the story goes that the icon of Durga was not made by man but just emerged on its own. Constructed in the eighteenth century it was dedicated to the Goddess Durga, the pond by the side was once connected to the river Ganges. The red 'paint' is more relevant when it is explained that it is representative of the deity Durga, and it is not Dulux, but an ochre, a naturally produced red pigment.

The monkeys are here in abundance, as are the signs warning you about them! The noises alone keep you on your toes, grip onto your hat and keep your bag fastened tight! It has been a good morning, two temples visited and while neither are in the must-see architecturally category, they have been interesting. We find our way back to the ghats in minutes, a herd of buffalos guiding us as they make their way down for a daily bath and scrub.

At the top of the steps a few ghats along we sit and enjoy a cup of chai at the Everest Café and have a bird's eye view looking down on all the action below. Slightly to our right are the buffalos, directly in front some laundry activity going on and a little further to the left we can see smoke coming from the funeral pyres. I am pretty certain that the smell of that laundry will not be recreated as a fabric conditioner fragrance any time soon!

Our afternoon is spent exploring the narrow lanes close to our digs, the night we arrived we never believed we would have got this brave! What we soon realised is that if you can find your way down to the river, making our way back to the Baba Guesthouse is easy. Cows are the biggest problems in these alleys, while locals just give them a shove, we are still a bit timid, almost apologising to the cow and hoping we soon reach a wider part where we can pass. Monkeys are also an issue, jumping from building to building, but also crapping from a great height; we originally thought we had a close encounter, dodged a bullet if you like, but soon realise that Alison is modelling the latest in monkey poo on the sleeve of her T-shirt.

As we make the short distance back home the drums of a wedding party are getting louder and louder, we even see the wedding horse, all decorated up and covered in intricate rugs (throws?), but unfortunately no sign of the wedding party. They must be in a courtyard somewhere within the labyrinth of passageways around here, we were interested in seeing what was going on.

By night we do not wander to far, having seen the Aarti ceremony the previous night we just head out for some food at the Baba restaurant. Once again vegetarians for the night, very much doubt meat free options back home are this tasty. It is a bonus that the Wi-Fi is really good, so we have a catch up with family and then head back to our room to kill some bugs and relax.

1st March

A restless night, a combination of insects and mosquitoes in the room and a change of bedding arrangement in the middle of the night. We swap the sheet from the mattress around with our furry overthrow and sleep much better. It was at this point that we cancelled the impending alarm setting to get up for the sunrise, that can wait until tomorrow.

Breakfast is a leisurely affair at the Baba restaurant, we have ticked the boxes of everything that we wanted to do here in Varanasi, today can be an unrushed wander along the ghats, down the alleys and passages, who knows what we will discover?

This morning seems to be the day of the stoned Babas; our idea of a Baba is a holy man, living a devout and basic life, maybe even reclusive, these guys look the part - saffron coloured robes, long beards etc. That is where the similarities end, the ones we see were either stoned, asking for cigarettes, or charging people to have their photographs taken; and with not being smokers we were happy to pay the twenty rupees for a snap! Perhaps some of them are into the spirituality of the place but many are there for the photo opportunities and the 'guru Dakshina', money to me and you! To be fair it is great to see them about, they add colour, mystery and another dimension to the place – and just because they are no longer matching our pre-conceived idea, does it really matter...

We carry on walking, looking to find our way beyond the Manikarnika ghat, the main burning place. Because of the nature of the place, you cannot just walk through it, yet the ghats by the river go way past here if we can find our way through the passages and streets beyond. We give it our best shot, more cows and dogs, even goats, but it is also the main route to bring the bodies through and down to the river. We know we need to head away from the river and take a right turn for a hundred metres or so, then double back, but we only find dead ends, no pun intended. In the end we have to admit defeat.

With nothing much to do we take a coffee break before heading back towards our base, but then continue further until we reach the Harishchandra ghat, a body is just being taken down to the river for the ritual bathing. Curiosity gets the better of us, so we take a seat on a step a good distance away and watch the entire process.

The body is brought back up from the river and placed on an unlit pyre, the head is further blessed with water from the river and the mourners walk around the body, a good number of times. The pyre is lit and the flames soon flare up and consume the body; before long, the feet that were pointing upwards in the twelve o' clock position flop around to point at the five and seven. The melting fat and sinew feeds the flames, at speed too. One of the workers from the ghat folds back in an arm that has dropped down to one side, poking it back into the trunk area. The feet eventually drop off and the ghat worker folds the rest of the legs into the chest, we guess the skin, ligaments and muscles have all gone by now so the body can be moved at his will.

It is surprising just how quick the entire process is, the shrouded body to a folded pile of bones in around an hour, we are told that it takes a further four hours for the bones to be ash and then the staff from the ghat just sweep the ash remains of the flesh and bones into the river. That is the same river that people are using for their daily ablutions, their laundry; there is little wonder why the river Ganges is one of the most polluted bodies of water in the world.

At the Everest Café we talk about what we have just seen, neither of us found it gruesome. It is far more graphic than what we do with our deceased back home, but it still has the same sense of ritual that we put into our services. Life, and death, in many parts of India really do happen in full view of everyone, it is just a completely unique way of life to what we take for granted. The buffaloes return for their evening bathe...

2nd March

The alarm wakes us from what has been a better night's sleep. It might be early but there are already lots of people about, and plenty of monkeys too... The sunrise has been worth getting up for, and the river has a lovely glow shining on it. The boat trips are running sunrise trips, is there any time of the day when they are not running? For us it is just a case of taking a few photos before returning to our room and packing our bags.

By seven o' clock we are checking out of the Baba Guesthouse, the man from reception leads us through the network of passageways; past the cows and their deposits plus a pair of dead rats. We soon reach the main road where Babaloo, the same guy who brought us here, is waiting for us. Goodbyes and our thanks are passed on before we head to the airport, hopefully missing the morning rush hour.

It is a smooth departure from Varanasi airport; no delays and no baggage to check in, time to sit down and enjoy our biscuits. On our transfer at Hyderabad airport, security must be bored, they make us switch on all our battery-operated items and check that all our plugs do actually provide power. It is a first for us, but better to be on the safe side rather than the security be lax. By this point we are hungry and there is a KFC in the departure halls, so that will do nicely for lunch; we also manage to 'obtain' a good supply of chilli sauce sachets for our egg butties, we had been running low!

There is a small delay before we get to board, but with a troupe of clowns wandering around the airport performing magic tricks for both children and adults that extra waiting time whizzes by. Once sat on the plane there is a further hold up, while a technical issue is sorted, maybe an elastic band is frayed - we are back on a propeller driven plane again. Hopefully nothing too serious... With that resolved it is time to fasten our seatbelts, take off and head up into the skies for our return to Goa.

Top row: The Ghats and the very old world a street or two back

Second: Baba, stoned or not, it's hard to tell, random cow in the alleyways and local barber

Third: Cows, goats and dogs, the Aarti ceremony and buffalo bath time...

Bottom: The Harishchandra cremation ghat and sunrise on the Ganges

A Last Few Days in Goa

March

We both wake up with fuzzy heads. A few too many drinks in Madhu's last night, we were still on a high after visiting Varanasi, and drank faster and more than normal...

Our trip is reaching it is close, we have seen everywhere and everything that we intended to, no mishaps or disasters – all that is left is for us to enjoy the beach and sun for the next ten days. Feelings are mixed; in some ways we are ready for home, seeing family and friends again, but on the other hand we had put so much time and effort into planning this adventure that we are sad that it is nearly over. Reality is that we need to be searching for jobs on our return to England. Anyway, enough of that for now...

Maybe it is with having been away for a few days that we notice how much hotter and humid it has become. Our conclusions are drawn after a morning trip to the market and an afternoon cooking; the ceiling fan in the kitchen is just swirling around stifling air, the decision is made, no more cooking for evening meals! The extra heat hasn't stopped us developing colds as we've both been a little 'sniffy' the last few days.

Days on the beach are now just sweltering and oppressive, the breeze of January and February seems to have disappeared. Dipping into the sea to cool off is not so pleasant either – there is tiny little jellyfish in places, nothing too painful but you can definitely feel them! Lunches of salad and chips are still good though and a Rovers Return Sunday roast was once again a reminder of home. Despite the beach vendors pestering us daily we still have not bought a selfie-stick!

We spend a great afternoon in Madhu's, by chance we get chatting with a lovely Indian couple, Wishy and Meena from Haryana, close to Delhi. Wishy speaks perfect English, it sounds like he is very well travelled, Meena is a little shy, but her language skills are also good. As the conservation flows it seems that they were friends of Steve Irwin, the deceased Australian zookeeper / environmentalist – his family is visiting them for an annual celebration in September, a trip they make every year. They give us a cashew fruit to try, it is like an apple, only smaller; a strange taste, almost sweet initially but with a sour after effect. It sounds like they have been scrumped from an old childhood stomping ground! We were only planning to stay for a couple of drinks but they insist upon more drinks and crisps, their treat; it sounds like they don't usually drink at all but are enjoying the freedom that Goa offers! It turns into the full afternoon and before saying goodbyes we exchange email addresses; they look a little wobbly as they set off walking back to their hotel...

It has got to the stage where we are having to choose carefully on where we eat each night, with only a handful of meals left we need to plan what dish where, we would hate to run out of evenings and miss out on a favourite! Drinking at night is always at Madhu's, by now we are never alone as we have become friends with so many other couples, although some of them are beginning to leave for home (many have been here since November). Goodbyes are said to Mike and Sylvia, a fantastic down to earth Yorkshire couple who share our love of Whitby. Ken and Mo are still here, though they have had an eventful time – Mo has been fitted with a stent after having a heart attack on the beach one day. Amazingly she was in and out of hospital in a matter of days and carrying on her holiday as if nothing happened within the week. Chef is a permanent fixture, supplying us with pate that is suitable for any meal – we have eaten it late at night, for breakfast and for a mid-afternoon snack!

The day before we depart our morning is spent giving the apartment a very thorough clean, final bits of washing and then a last trip to the market to purchase gifts for Valerie, Savio and Sovann. The treat for Valerie is a little strange, she loves bananas. The chocolate is for Savio and Sovann, we think they are addicted to the stuff, plus a big cake from a local bakery. We get to sample the cake ourselves later as Savio knocks on our door and insists that we come to the shop for the slicing ceremony!

The final night in Madhu's and its goodbyes all around. We will miss Chef - he is entertaining in different ways at different times. By afternoon he is great company, incredibly wise and knowledgeable, full of stories from his early years growing up in Mumbai, a keen backgammon player and a superb cook. By night he can rub some people up the wrong way, often blunt, but always amusing – we will miss his 'Yabba-Dabba-Do' Fred Flintstone impressions whenever a particularly attractive young Russian lady walks by!

Homeward Bound

12th March

Packing our bags for the final time does not take long. It is a strange morning, lots of clock watching – just killing time until our quarter past eleven pick up.

The keys for the apartment are handed back to Valerie, fortunately she had called Mr Diego earlier to confirm our collection time and he had forgotten all about us! More goodbyes and then the short journey to the airport. Every other time we have left Goa it has been on a flight departing in the early hours of the morning, and often been chaotic – today is so much more relaxed, we are soon checked in and with our baggage offloaded there's just immigration to navigate.

The flight to Muscat is a mixed bag, it is our first ever flight with Oman Air. Legroom is a bit lacking, and we are both short! The in-flight entertainment options are good though and the foods passable, for some reason Alison gets a 'special' meal, why will remain a mystery. On arrival we go straight to the Transfer Services desk and join another English couple who have had the same flight amendments made, the lady at the desk deals with us all at the same time.

The minibus takes us to the Goldon Tulip Hotel, it is situated just outside the confines of the airport and first impressions are one of sheer luxury. Reception advises us that we have meal vouchers for both this evening and breakfast tomorrow morning, and with that it is off to find our rooms. Twin beds but with fluffy duvets and nice linen, the bathroom is huge and nicely fitted out, all very opulent compared to the places that we have stayed for the last four months or so. The evening meal options are endless, buffet style so we have the full three courses... not really knowing what to go for as neither of us are that familiar with Middle Eastern cuisine.

13th March

What a night's sleep! The beds were so plush, the duvet so soft, the air-conditioning so quiet; one of the best we have had for a long while.

The breakfast spread was huge, our biggest problem was that we were not that hungry. Last night's food was delicious, big thumbs up from us, but we ate too much! We have a lighter breakfast, opting for a lot of the fruit options, disappointed that we cannot manage more, it looks so good. A walk around the hotel's garden to stretch our legs, today will involve a lot of sitting. There is not that much to see, but the lawns and gardens are immaculate.

Reception is quiet; we wait and chat with the other English couple who are on the same flight, they were asking us about Vietnam as that is where they are planning to visit next year. They have just spent most of this winter in Goa, and really enjoyed it, but are looking for a more active trip next time around – Vietnam certainly fits that brief.

Our pick-up is on time, a swift five-minute journey to the airport. Through passport control and then THREE bag checks before we are straight to our boarding gate. It looks like the flight is already being loaded, everyone is stood and the queue is long, it looks like it is a free for all, rather than done by row numbers. One final check of the passport and ticket before making our way down to the bus, that will take us to the plane, that will soon depart for Heathrow....

Epilogue

Firstly, apologies for any changes of tense, this has all been revisited through Alison's original diary from the trip and has subsequently been written up by both of us. Hopefully that accounts for any changes in the pattern or style of what you have just read and hasn't detracted from our story.

We hope you enjoyed the read of our time away, and perhaps it has brought back memories of your own times spent in this fantastic part of the world? If you have never explored Asia and are considering giving it a go, then go for it! We made unforgettable memories, saw amazing sights, and had the time of our lives (we just never realised how much eating and drinking we did along the way). With the internet and a little research anything is possible, so if you have a dream go follow it.

What was next for us? Upon returning home we both lasted twelve weeks in the first jobs we took! Our second jobs lasted two years, they were ok but neither of us found them rewarding or challenging compared to the previous positions we had held before redundancy changed our paths. In December 2018 we both handed in our notices and once more went travelling again. We had enjoyed the experience that you have just read about so much that in January 2019 we revisited Cambodia and then spent a further three months exploring Vietnam, dropping in places that we had flown over last time.

Bangkok was once again our starting point, but this time in the backpacker streets of Kho San Road (a crazy experience). Travel and accommodation were even more budget this time, not due to finances but more a testament of how much we had enjoyed the company of younger travellers we had met last time. Every one of the near three thousand miles (4,800km) would be on land; by bus and a single train journey, accommodation in a mix of guesthouses and hostels, private room but with shared facilities on occasions.

The year 2020 took us to Malaysia and Borneo, again on a budget. We even did our first ever dormitory stay while visiting the Kinabatangan River in Borneo, what a place that is, we were fortunate enough to see a wild orangutan making his bed for the night. Then came the Covid-19 epidemic... After a near three-year hiatus, we are heading back to Malaysia to finish off what we started, taking in Singapore for a few days along the way.

Travel is an infectious bug, we now have more countries on our list to visit than ever before, hopefully many more dreams to be fulfilled...

Also in this series...

Our Travels Around India

A trip to India is not as one dimensional as sight alone. It is an assault on all your senses, the sounds of the constantly parping horns from the traffic, shouts of 'taxi?' as you walk by a card-playing driver and the honk or bell of the bread man selling his bakes. The smells, both good and bad, the rotting rubbish somewhere near the bottom of the spectrum and the aroma of fantastic food most definitely at the top. Spices, and the smells coming from the restaurants suitably bring us on to taste. For lovers of Indian cuisine, you are immediately transported to food heaven, if spicy curries are not your bag, then the apple pie and ice cream from Infantaria is equally divine. Working our way through all the senses, the touch must be that of the sand between your toes as you walk carefree along the beach... far better than the gritty feeling it has once it is in your bed when you wake up next morning, having trailed it there from the dusty roads the night before!

What initially attracted us to the country was the food, neither of us can get enough of it, be that the afternoon snacks of samosas, batata wadas or the endless curry dish options in the evening! So, for us a holiday where you can indulge in your favourite meals is perfect. It might seem strange to many but we are not beach people; we both love the idea of relaxing on a sunbed for hours on end, just reading or people watching, but the reality is that after two or three days of that we are bored and restless. We concluded that to enjoy the best of both worlds we would book a fortnights holiday to Goa, but then also have a 'plan,' something away from the coast for a few days that would also be a tick on the bucket list.

Over the years we have visited the Golden Triangle, taking in Delhi, Agra and Jaipur. We loved Jaipur so much that we subsequently made a second visit to Rajasthan and explored Jodhpur and Udaipur, an incredibly beautiful city that was quite serene and a pleasure to wander around. Changes to our return connecting flight in Mumbai meant that we had to tag on an additional day there! From Goa a single but long train journey into Karnataka to visit Hampi gave us another memorable few days away in a place we had never even heard of! Kerala was a tour and beach stay; a rice boat on the backwaters of Alleppey and the city of Cochin before heading to the hills to visit the tea plantations. We got to experience a home stay before moving on to visit Periyar National Park. From the beach resort of Kovalum we arranged ourselves a trip down to the Southernmost tip of India, Kanyakumari.

We also visited the other end of the country, Amritsar! What a place this is, most famous as the home of the Sikh pilgrimage site of the Golden Temple but also a place of shame from our colonial past, the massacre at Jallianwala Bagh. Close to Amritsar is the most joyous place we have ever visited in India; the Wagah border ceremony is a must see. Every night is party night at this crazy border closing ceremony as Pakistan and Indian soldiers try to outdo each other in moustaches, high kicking marches and posturing – all in front of dancing, chanting high-energy crowds. Mysore and its stunning palace (via a one-night stay in Bangalore), was our destination to break up our stay another year. In 2016 we finally made our way to Varanasi, it had always been a tricky one to reach due to flight connection times, but in our two months stay we had no excuses not to make it. It more than lived up to expectations, a truly fascinating place.

Printed in Great Britain
by Amazon